I Wis
Strategies a...
Best! Bruce Nelson

RESTAURANT MANAGEMENT

the Myth, the Magic, the Math

BRUCE NELSON

Minneapolis, Minnesota

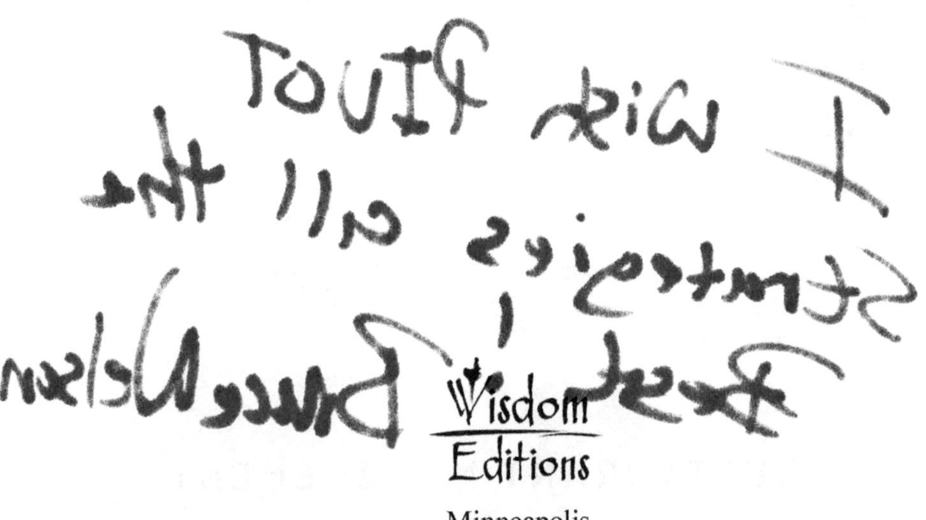

Minneapolis

SECOND EDITION DECEMBER 2022

Restaurant Management: The Myth, the Magic, the Math.

 Wisdom Editions is an imprint of Calumet Editions, LLC. For information, write to Calumet Editions, 6800 France Avenue South, Suite 370, Edina, MN 55435

10 9 8 7 6 5 4 3 2

ISBN: 978-1-959770-27-5

Cover design: Daniel West

Interior design: Gary Lindberg

Contents

RESTAURANT MANAGEMENT

the Myth, *the* Magic, *the* Math

I dedicate this book to my late father, Robert Lawrence Nelson, whose passion for restaurants was bestowed upon me at a very young age. His blueprint for serving excellent food and providing warm hospitality was present in all of my past restaurant adventures and his spirit will live on as part of every future restaurant I touch. Although I often rebelled, looking for the easier way out, the restaurant fundamentals my father taught me are timeless and unchanging.

Part One—The Myths

"I decided that it was not wisdom that enabled poets to write their poetry, but a kind of instinct or inspiration, such as you find in seers and prophets who deliver all their sublime messages without knowing in the least what they mean."

—Socrates[1]

It was the many myths of business ownership that lured this sailor into the jagged rocks of restaurant management. Throughout history, myths have been created out of truths uttered by people of prominence, reputation or respect. Myths are the adages that in themselves embody an invitation to ponder the truth of a concept for further meaning.

For example, a common myth perpetrated upon children by parents, teachers and mentors is this: "If you work hard, you will be successful." This "hard work = success" adage is a perfectly reasonable statement because its opposite, "slothfulness = failure" is true in most cases. After forty years of observation and experience, however, I can assure you that hard work in itself is no guarantee of restaurant success. Some of my "dream" restaurants floundered, yet others became successful. The question I asked myself was, "Why?" My work ethic was the same whether I failed or was successful.

The answer was simple: too often I had believed the myths imposed by the hardy stock of Swedes and Norwegians from the

Northwoods of Minnesota. If my restaurant was failing, I believed it must have been because I had ignored the "hard work = success" law canonized by nearly five centuries of Protestant reform. If I wished to become successful, the Puritan work ethic demanded that I cast out my sins, subdue all forms of earthly passions, and work harder!

Another great myth uttered by those clinging to the side of the cliff is the old saying that "Failure is not an option." This may be a great motivational slogan for a coach during a halftime pep talk when the team is down by three touchdowns, but both coach and the lads know that failure is indeed an option—and being down by twenty-one points at halftime, a more *likely* outcome! Statistically, among independent restaurant upstarts, failure is a highly probable outcome. After all, most stories of epic failure are retold on the couches of therapists and the barstools of local taverns, not canonized in restaurant journals and feature films.

First-time restaurant owners are like the novices sitting at the poker table with a full boat, queens over aces, grinning ear to ear as they go all in. They are so convinced they have been dealt a winning hand that a lifeboat is unnecessary. Because they have dreamed about their new restaurant venture for so long and they have worked so hard to get to the table, they become convinced that their hand will take the jackpot. Enthusiasm, self-assurance, planning and skill are all great components for launching a successful restaurant. But the myth that "failure is not an option" falls woefully short when life is holding four kings!

Another restaurant myth is that location dictates success. Yes, a good location makes greater success more probable. But in the twenty-first century, both real estate developers and landlords are hip to this emphasis on location and are not shy about placing a premium price tag on choice locations. Poorly run restaurants in great locations still fail. Well-run restaurants in unlikely or undesirable locations do succeed. In fact, I often see first-time restaurants succeed in the most unlikely locations.

Myth Four: "Serve good food and they will come." The power of this myth seduces many talented chefs into opening their own restaurants. The "build it and they will come" myth makes for great Hollywood drama, as portrayed in the film *A Field of Dreams*, but in the real world, serving really good food has very little to do with running a successful restaurant. This doesn't mean that serving crappy food is the recipe for success, but I can point to many successful restaurants that serve mediocre food. A well-run restaurant with tight operational controls and a menu priced for profit will financially outperform the best chef-driven restaurant that is clueless about food and overhead costs. After all, both types of restaurants attract customers looking for a good meal.

Have you ever stumbled upon a little gem of a restaurant in a nondescript strip mall near your home? The food is excellent, the owners are present every time you visit, and perhaps you have been there so often the owner knows you by name. Maybe you attend the same church and your children play on the same soccer team. Over the course of time, your favorite neighborhood restaurant gets busier. On Friday and Saturday nights, even you—one of their first and most loyal customers— wait in line for a table. You may even stop going to the restaurant, uttering those famous words spoken by Yogi Berra, "Nobody goes there anymore… it's too crowded." Then some time passes, and you find yourself jonesing for that particular dish at your old neighborhood haunt. It's midweek, so you surmise you'll be able to get a table. You pull into the strip mall and walk up to the door only to find a sign—"Restaurant Closed." How could this restaurant close? The food was so good, the owners were so nice, our kids played soccer together. What could have gone wrong? Well, what went wrong was that your favorite restaurant fell prey to the myth that serving good food was the sole key to success. The restaurant failed because the owners did not know how to model the business for sustained profit.

This next myth, "having deep pockets," is one of my favorites. It's the false idea that having ample funds to build a restaurant will assure success. When someone approaches me about their dream of opening a restaurant, I usually offer this reply: "I know how to make a small fortune in the restaurant business… start with a large fortune!" Although I will never minimize the importance of starting a business venture with adequate funding, either your own capital or favorable financing, but that alone does not guarantee success. Sometimes the opposite occurs— the confidence of deep pockets and adequate resources to fund initial losses can cause you to fail to adapt quickly enough to an unprofitable restaurant model. Whether funding comes from institutional financing or a rich uncle, neither will accept continuing losses and the dreaded cash calls on your failing business model. The reality for startup restaurateurs is that having limited resources forces you to make necessary changes to the business model more quickly, which is a good thing.

I have written this book for all those who have laid all their chips on the table only to find that a royal flush beats a full boat. I will teach you that if you set up a model for managing profit, your restaurant dreams do not have to be a gamble, and your opponent holding the royal flush does not have it in for you. The winning hand is just what happens when you learn to overcome the restaurant myths, focus on managing the restaurant magic and master the restaurant math!

In the Beginning...

How did I, Gen X baby, son of a teacher and a tombstone peddler, rack up more than forty years of restaurant experience? It began in 1969, when my father, Robert, sold the inherited shares from his father's tombstone business to Uncle Jim and purchased a hotel in Detroit Lakes, Minnesota. The Graystone Hotel was a classic small-town lodging across the street from the Great Northern Train Depot.

The Graystone Hotel

The Graystone was built in 1916 and was grander than any other building in a town known mainly as a fishing and hunting stop on the Great Northern Railroad. But by 1969, when my father purchased the hotel, it was in disrepair. Its small, non-air-conditioned rooms were no match for the multiple resorts that had popped up around Detroit Lakes. By the early 1970s, tourists much preferred quaint waterfront cottages to the drab brick hotel with lackluster views of Highway 10 and the train tracks. In fact, when my father purchased the hotel, it was in the middle of being converted into apartments. There was a smattering of long-term, mostly elderly hotel occupants, and the rest of the rooms were available for the Harold Hill-type drifters who meandered through town. In addition to the sleeping rooms, the hotel had a dining room, a coffee shop, and banquet rooms in a dingy, poorly lit basement. Although the economic viability of the hotel rooms and apartment rentals was questionable, my father saw promise in the food service, and thus began his journey as a restaurant man.

To a five-year-old kid, the hotel was a magical place. While my friends were outside riding bikes and throwing baseballs, I was wandering the halls of the Graystone Hotel and eating hamburgers in the coffee shop. My sister and I would ride the linen carts pushed by Ida, the hotel maid, and irritate the head chef, Ernie, a grumpy old man who loved fishing and drinking. Whenever the drinking got the better of Ernie, my father would fire him and step behind the line to do the cooking. When the cooking got the better of my father, he would rehire Ernie.

The Graystone Hotel had a rickety old Otis elevator, the kind where you would enter through the elevator doors and then shut a mechanical metal gate to engage the lift mechanism. At that time, the elevator was only one of two in the entire city of Detroit Lakes. Much to the chagrin of guests staying at the hotel, I would spend hours riding in the elevator and punching the buttons for all four floors.

Another fascinating feature of the old hotel was in the kitchen—a water-driven freight elevator that was an open carriage connected to a series of ropes. I would pull on one rope and hear water rushing as the elevator descended into the dreary basement. If I'd pull the other rope, the running water would propel the elevator back up to the kitchen.

Like John Irving's classic novel, *The Hotel, New Hampshire,* I lived the life of Egg, haplessly wandering about the hotel, clueless to the fact that I was a great annoyance to Ida, Ernie, and the hotel guests. To me, the Graystone Hotel was a giant playground, and I was oblivious to the fact that young children should not wander about a kitchen filled with meat grinders, slicers, knives and hot ovens.

Five years later, in 1974, my father sold the Graystone Hotel and bought a Country Kitchen restaurant franchise. Little Egg lost his playground but graduated to another form of entertainment. The restaurant was busy, and the sound of rock & roll played at every table as guests plugged tableside jukeboxes with quarters. Every pop song from 1974 to 1979 was permanently burned into my brain. I got so tired of hearing the Bee Gees that every time "Night Fever" played I'd run to the storeroom and kick the record playing machine, causing the song to skip and launch into the next one—which, sadly, was usually "Staying Alive."

It was at Country Kitchen where the restaurant bug caught me. I was only thirteen years old and had started washing dishes and busing tables during the summer months. By the time I was fourteen, I was cooking on the line. First, I mastered prep, and then eggs, hash browns, omelets, and the fryer. Then, I moved to the grill where I learned how to cook hamburgers and grilled sandwiches. By the time I was fifteen, I was running the line, calling out the orders and plating entrees. I also received the first of many battle scars while improperly cleaning a meat slicer.

I continued to hone my cooking skills throughout my high school years by following my father to the various other restaurants he ran. By the time I was eighteen, I was managing Detroit Country Club under my father's direction. I could now add cooking steaks and seafood to my repertoire, as well as bartending. On my eighteenth birthday, I poured my first legal drinks to golfers who were assembled at the club for "men's" day. Later that year I wrote my first dinner menu including the wine list. The hospitality bug had bitten me hard, and I was enjoying the thrill of considering myself a "restaurateur."

I would like to say that the "salad" days of my restaurant career were easy and profitable— but they were not. My father was a great cook and a wonderful front-of-the-house man. Locally, he had a great reputation for putting out good food, and guests flocked to his restaurants. But, at the end of the day (and at the end of the year) there was never much money left. To be honest, as a teenager, I couldn't understand why working hard did not translate into financial success. Chalk it up to youthful naïveté, but at this young age I assumed every business owner made money. That was the impression I had gathered from my parents' friends, most of whom were owners of local businesses.

It wasn't until the late 70s that I learned the reality that being a business owner is indeed fickle. It was at this time that my father leveraged his success running the local Country Kitchen into a franchise opportunity in Nevada. Then the economy fell into a deep recession, interest rates on business loans exceeded 21%, and Jimmy Carter was the Dark Lord who singlehandedly caused this business misery. I witnessed my father's business suffer along with those of his friends. The guy who sold snowmobiles and motorboats closed his doors. The man who sold ready-mix concrete greatly reduced his staff and started driving the mixer trucks himself. The friend who owned the grocery store sold his business to a local franchiser and left town.

By the time I entered high school, it had become apparent that the restaurant business consisted chiefly of long hours, hard work and low pay. Nobody worked harder than my father for so little reward. I know this because I worked side-by-side with him for the same low reward. Despite the pay, I enjoyed working in my father's restaurants. I enjoyed cooking, the camaraderie and family-like atmosphere amongst the staff, and I enjoyed serving customers. But I knew there was a gap in my financial knowledge. Though I knew how to cook and how to generate sales, I simply didn't know how to make money operating restaurants. And so, I enrolled at Hamline University with a major in Business Administration.

No one story could possibly encapsulate all the joys, adventures and frustrations that a restaurateur experiences, nor can it touch on all the lessons learned and philosophical insights gained. The stories in this book chronicle not so much my spiritual transformation, but how I developed a true understanding of restaurant finance. However, before I can show you where the journey took me, I must share with you some of the rough seas I traversed.

The Unraveling of a Dream

"Transformation isn't sweet and bright. It's a dark and murky, painful pushing. An unraveling of the untruths you've carried in your body. A practice in facing your own created demons. A complete uprooting, before becoming."

—Victoria Erickson

In the summer of 2001 my third child was only three months old, I was three months behind on my mortgage payments, my ten-year-old BMW had just thrown a timing belt, and the restaurant I had spent years dreaming about and over two years designing and building was swimming in a sea of red ink. Vendors were hounding me for payment. Deliveries, if I could get them, were cash on delivery (COD), and I had no idea how I was going to make the next payroll. My business partner had pulled the plug on additional funding, and I had burned through all possible assistance from family members. Like my rickety old sailboat, my life was in shambles, and I was barely able to stay afloat.

On top of being a father to three children under the age of five, I was on the verge of the bank foreclosing on my home and my restaurant, vendors launching lawsuits for past-due bills, and dealing with extremely strained family relationships. If all this was not enough, in the spring of 2001 I had also realized that I had an addiction to alcohol. So, my wife hated me, my parents were mad at me, my business partners had given up on me, my CPA ignored me, the city council which had gave me a sweetheart deal on the land for my restaurant turned its back on me, my friends didn't know what to do to help me, and alcohol—the one damn thing that had gotten me through each day—had betrayed me. The only two individuals who were not entirely disgusted with me were the town sheriff, who served me my daily lawsuit notices, and my banker, who was in the process of foreclosing on my restaurant.

Rest assured, however, this book is not a tale of alcoholism and recovery. It is a story of arrogance, epic business failure and, most importantly, spiritual and financial recovery. The painful revelation of my addiction had merely occurred simultaneously with the revelation that there was nothing I could do to save my dream restaurant. I did, however, blame my addiction on the restaurant's failure. I even sent out a newsletter stating that my problem drinking was why I had to close the restaurant instead of stating the simple truth that my restaurant had run out of money because I didn't know what I was doing. I did wonder, though, if my addiction was a factor. It was sort of a "chicken and egg" issue. Did I fail at running my restaurant because of my addiction, or did I become addicted because I was failing at running a restaurant?

But it didn't matter. The reason my business failed is that, though I had succeeded in creating the magic that drew customers to my restaurant, I had fallen prey to the myths of entrepreneurialism and entirely failed to understand the math.

Who in the World Would Do This?

In 2004, after washing out as a restaurant owner, I took a job as a chef instructor at a culinary school. My job was to teach "Intro to Culinary Arts," which was a practicum of basic cooking skills, knife skills and sanitation. On the first day of class, I always asked my students to introduce themselves and explain why they were in my class. Nearly 90 percent of them said the reason they wanted to learn how to cook was that they dreamed of opening a restaurant someday.

In 2004, many celebrity chefs were making a name for themselves on television. Cooking shows were gaining popularity as a reality TV genre. Gaining chef notoriety was a little hard for me to comprehend, because when I graduated from high school in 1984, the only celebrity chef on TV was Julia Child. Although she was adorable, her quirky style and distinctive voice served mostly as fodder for parody not motivation for opening a restaurant. Thus, those of us who gravitated toward the restaurant business in the mid-80s, did so for the love of the industry and the thrill of adventure. The thought of becoming a restaurant celebrity prior to the "celebrity chef" era was nonexistent.

I found it interesting, however, that most of my young students wanted to open their own restaurants. And it wasn't just the culinary students. Throughout my forty years in the restaurant industry, most sous chefs, executive chefs, bar managers and general managers I have met harbor the same dream—to one day own a restaurant.

The "restaurant owning" impulse amongst hospitality professionals is very powerful, like the dream of young thespians to have their names on the theater marquee. (A side note to all existing restaurant owners—there is a lot of creative energy in your existing team members who grind out fifty to sixty hours a week running your stores. Learn to tap into their energy and reward them, or they may become your next competitor. And, unlike the stranger opening a restaurant next to you, your managers know all your weaknesses.)

I was certainly one of those dreaming general managers. Over the course of my career, I have drawn up plans for over a dozen different restaurant concepts that I one day hoped to open. Interestingly, the restaurants I designed followed my age and entertainment interests. In my twenties I designed hip cocktail joints; in my thirties I leaned toward worldly culinary-type restaurants; in my forties I designed restaurants for stability. Now, as a 50-year-old restaurant CFO, the restaurant dreams swirling in my head have to do with establishing a legacy. Restaurateurs are always dreaming about restaurants, and no sooner do they open the doors on one when the next great concept starts bursting into their heads.

So, who is the restaurant-owning type? Not an individual who seeks financial success and stability. Those types end up in the banking, finance and government sectors. It's not individuals seeking a Monday through Friday 9-to-5 job. That type of individual ends up in corporate settings. It definitely isn't individuals who seek to balance work, family and leisure time. That type ends up selling insurance or working in academics. Restaurateurs have a passion for serving and a drive to work the hours required to meet that passion. True restaurateurs' family time and leisure time are wrapped into the restaurants. My own children were born into the restaurants I was running. From the time they could walk, they were part of my restaurant's fabric. To this day, we still take our meals together in the restaurants I serve.

I believe that most people drawn to restaurant ownership are drawn to the freedom they perceive it will allow. They are drawn to the freedom of designing and serving menu items of their choosing, and to the freedom of not being told what to do and when to do it. They are drawn to the freedom of being their own bosses. Although no restaurant owners put their life on the line without the hope of becoming financially successful, I contend that material wealth is not the reason why people decide to own restaurants. There is just a mystique about being a restaurant owner. Images of Rick in the movie *Casablanca* come to mind—the smooth-talking saloon owner in a smart dinner jacket who is quick to light a pretty girl's cigarette and reluctant to share a bourbon with any unsavory guests. Or Tony Soprano's lifelong friend, Artie Bucco, owner of Nuovo Vesuvio on *The Sopranos*. There are many great movies that romanticize restaurant ownership—*Ratatouille*, *The Hundred–Foot Journey*, *The Big Night* and *Tortilla Soup* are just a few. My point is that hundreds of movies and television shows center around the entertainment factor that is the hospitality industry. Alas, these entertainment icons perpetuate another myth that draws people to restaurant ownership—that restaurant ownership is sexy!

Those of us who get into this business have a vision in our minds of who we want to be. The one thing we don't envision is that we are Gordon Gekko of *Wall Street* fame, master manipulator of high finance and money markets. People who dream of serving good food and drink and being hospitable to complete strangers are not primarily driven by greed. By the very essence of what it takes to run a restaurant, greed is abandoned, because first and foremost, people who work in the industry have already agreed to give up that which is most precious and ultimately limited. People who love to work in the restaurant industry give up their time in pursuit of their dream. Very few other industries demand so much time, and the ones that do, like attorneys or doctors, are usually highly compensated for their sacrifice. Not so for the restaurant manager working ten-to-twelve hour shifts six days a week, working nights, weekends, and holidays. Anyone who is greedy with their time would never be foolish enough to get into the restaurant business, and the ones who are tend to fail quickly.

It is important to get into the mindset of why someone would want to become a restaurant owner. Without understanding the internal makeup of a restaurateur, I cannot start laying out the myths of restaurant ownership, the magic that truly makes restaurants desirable, and the math that makes the dream of restaurant ownership sustainable.

Part Two—The Magic

"Never tell the audience how good you are. They will soon find out for themselves."

—Harry Houdini

Magic is what hospitality entrepreneurs build. Magic is the thumping base and neon lights of a late-night club. Magic is the quaint sidewalk café overlooking an urban park. Magic is the smell of saddle soap, leather and whiskey at a Western barbecue joint. Magic is polished waitstaff and silverware in a restaurant where it takes over a month to get a reservation. Magic is the sixty-year-old supper club where the unchanged décor has now become retro-chic. Magic is the dive bar filled with so much nostalgia and tackiness that it draws in customers rather than repels them. Restaurateurs create magic, the inviting atmospheres that draw customers in to spend their time and money enjoying carefully crafted experiences.

One of the biggest mistakes restaurateurs make is believing that their restaurant's purpose is solely to provide their customers with food and drink. Indeed, I used to believe that, and so do most chefs and entrepreneurs who take a chance on opening their very own restaurants. That is why so many new restaurants open with excellent, chef-driven food and wonderful, well-thought-out craft cocktails. I have been around long enough to watch many of these fresh new concepts open to great fanfare and positive reviews from both professional and amateur foodies only to see the vast majority close within eighteen months. Great food and drinks are a component of restaurants, but not their sole raison d'être. After all, if customers simply wanted a well-aged scotch, a barrel-aged bourbon, an excellent craft beer, or an elite Bordeaux, they could simply acquire those products at a much cheaper price and enjoy them in the comfort of their own home. Although it requires a slightly better skill set, it is cheaper to acquire the ingredients for your favorite meal and cook it yourself at home. I realize that time and skill are factors, but the reality is that customers choose restaurants not only to satisfy their appetites but to have wonderful experiences.

Restaurants, bars, nightclubs, cafés and every concept in between are manufacturers of experiences. Like every other manufacturing company, restaurants are comprised of a physical plant, production staff, delivery staff, sales agents, and management to oversee the process and marketing of the business. The experience is what customers are paying for, and that experience includes indulging the five senses of human perception with music, lighting and artwork, textures, aromas and tastes all accompanied by well-trained waitstaff and bartenders. Successful restaurants must manufacture a culture that stimulates those five senses while operating within a model that makes a profit.

In fairness to all the teachers out there, there are simply some lessons that cannot be taught solely by theoretical examples. Like, for example, instructing your teenager to proceed cautiously and give greater distance to the car in front of them when driving in icy conditions. Though the theoretical lesson may leave a faint imprint in their brain, nothing drives home the lesson more permanently than slamming on the brakes as they approach an intersection and experience the helplessness of their car slowly sliding into the vehicle in front of them. I will illustrate how I came to understand the basic tenants of the myths, the magic and the math as I chronicle some of my own restaurant missteps. It always seemed as though the mistakes I made appeared as suddenly as that car in front of me on an icy road, but in retrospect the challenges had been there all along, and I could've avoided the slow-motion accidents that followed.

Magic to the Extreme!

Every restaurateur has the one that got away, the concept that has been percolating in their minds for years. In a lot of ways, a restaurateurs are like sailors. They are happy to ride along in any ship, but they dream of the one boat they will call their own, the grand vessel they will captain. For me, these dreams became most vivid when the work was most bleak.

My ship was Portofino. I dreamed of her on and off for over ten years. There were many Saturday nights, after cleaning up after a long day, that the dream of Portofino kept me from throwing my apron at the owner and walking out the door. Dreaming of Portofino was my lifeline during the part of my career where my knowledge and efforts made other owners lots of money but left me woefully unfulfilled. I dreamed of taking the helm of my own ship and reaping the spoils of my own conquest.

In 1998 I was in my twentieth year of restaurant operations. I was running the suite level of Target Center in downtown Minneapolis. The job was to facilitate the service of food and beverage to sixty-eight corporate suites and over two thousand people within a 45-minute timeframe. As General Manager, I worked directly with the ownership to manage budgets and profitability. Prior to Target Center, I had worked for a large independent Italian eatery, bakery and grocery store in St. Paul. In that capacity I had also worked directly with the owner to establish budgets and maintain profitability. Over the preceding twenty years, I had owned two of my own businesses and worked as a catering sales manager for a large Minneapolis catering operation. Although I understood that my Target Center job was to help the owners achieve and maintain profitability, I pined for the day that I could open my own restaurant. That desire plus twenty years of experience had led me to believe that I was ready to be my own captain.

In the spring of 1998, when I decided to leave my comfortable job, pull up stakes in St. Paul and return to my hometown to open Portofino Restaurant & World Market, I was thirty-three years old, married, and had a fifteen-month-old daughter with a second child on the way. I lived in a drafty old Victorian home off Summit Avenue in St. Paul, Minnesota, and had been a general manager for various Twin Cities operations for nearly a decade. My evenings consisted of coming home after a long day of work, pouring myself several stiff cocktails and complaining to my wife about how hard I worked and how underappreciated I was. My wife, who had been dealing with the antics of a 15-month-old child in addition to being pregnant, finally snapped and said, "If you hate your job so much, quit. Go open a new restaurant!"

Pounding down my third stiff martini, I concluded—dammit, I'll do it. Thus, on a cold spring evening in 1998, with snow still on the ground, I made the decision to build my dream restaurant and become my own boss.

The big question was where my brilliant new restaurant was going to be located. Both my wife and I had roots in Detroit Lakes,

Minnesota. I was born and raised there, and my wife's grandfather owned a cottage a few doors down from my ancestral lake home. We both had fond memories of our youthful summers in Detroit Lakes and believed that community would be the ideal place to give raise our children. Besides, that is where my father's reputation as a restaurant man still carried some weight, and it was the place where I started my restaurant career and achieved a modicum of success ten years ago with Dunnvilla Supper Club. In hindsight, I know it was the martini talking, but at the time moving to Detroit Lakes to open a restaurant made perfect sense.

I made it known in my hometown of Detroit Lakes that I was interested in purchasing a restaurant. If you know anything about resort towns in north country, restaurants sink or swim during the narrow time in the summer when lake residents and vacationers appear. It is a very fickle business, and like farming, restaurant owners in Detroit Lakes pray that Zephyrus, the God of gentle west winds, will blow the tourists into town to fill the restaurant chairs.

I entered negotiations with three prominent restaurants. All three restaurants were asking well over market for their well-known but tired concepts. Two of them could not produce financial statements that came close to supporting their asking prices. Those of you who have been in this business know the drill. The owner of a restaurant produces a P&L (Profit and Loss) statement that shows the establishment breaking even, or maybe losing a little bit of money. Then they proceed to tell you how much money they really make (wink-wink, nudge-nudge.) Personally, I've yet to find a banker who accepts the wink-wink/nudge-nudge business pro forma.

So, after lamenting to my CPA that I could not find a business to buy in my hometown, he pointed out that the city of Detroit Lakes had just acquired a piece of property on the public beach and was looking for a specific retail business to occupy that space. He told me the asking price was around $175,000 for the one-acre parcel. I joked with him, "Hell, I could buy that land and build a restaurant on it for less money than those restaurant owners were asking for their tired businesses." That throw-away conversation kicked off the development of my baby—the boat of my dreams—the lady dubbed and christened Portofino Restaurant & World Market.

I was able to secure the land from the city and spent the next year designing, building and opening my dream. I was only thirty-three years old, but I'd been in the restaurant business for over twenty years. I'd worked for some of the most successful restaurateurs in the Minneapolis-St. Paul area as a general manager. Although I had never occupied the position of chef, I was a good cook and had a great palate. I had spent countless hours designing and costing menus. I had overseen construction of new restaurants as well as remodeled various establishments. I had put together several business pro formas and knew how to secure bank financing.

I truly believed I was walking into this business opportunity with the experience, knowledge and motivation needed to be successful. And indeed, when I finally opened the doors in June 2000, we were so wildly busy that I don't believe I took a day off during the first six weeks. The early days of Portofino were a lot of fun. The guests enjoyed the atmosphere, the menu proved to be successful at bringing customers through the doors and, my God, did we sell a lot of wine. A solid wine program was an integral part of the Portofino concept, but I had no idea how starved this little part of western Minnesota was for decent wines. I believe my original pro forma called for about 10 percent of my sales in wine. The reality was that about 25 percent of overall sales were from wine.

Then, as always happens in the resort havens of northwestern Minnesota, Zephyrus gave up the ghost. September came, and the lake homes began to go dormant. October came as the ducks and geese began to fly south. November arrived with the leaves falling to the ground and the north winds blowing in the chill that would soon turn to snow. Christmas came and went, along with the retirees dubbed "snowbirds," who were off to the warm climes and tax retreats of Florida, Texas and Arizona. With these changes of seasons, a new reality hit home. Debt payments still needed to be made on time. Payroll still came around every two weeks. Vendors still had a notion that they should be paid on time for their delivered products. From the high season of summer to the low season of January I got slapped upside the head by the reality that my dream might prove to be a nightmare.

Though the dream of Portofino was my emotional lifeline, nine months into operations I needed a financial lifeline. What occurred at this point, and my subsequent actions, is the impetus for this book. But before we get to my solution, let me finish the tale of Portofino.

Calling SOS!

Portofino had been operating for about nine months. The restaurant was awash in red ink, and tensions were strained between myself and my partner/investor. That investor had already put in a six-figure cash infusion to help Portofino limp to the end of the year. Now, it was three months later, and the another six-figure cash call was required to repair our ship and keep her afloat so we could reap the rewards of the summer tourist season. My investor, rightly so, was not keen on the idea of another unequal cash call.

After much stress and strain, a family member agreed to supply the funds required to keep Portofino operating until summer. When she handed me the check, she looked in my eyes and said, "You can make this thing work, right?" It had never occurred to me that given time I wouldn't make this business successful. Alas, ego and fear are toxic bedfellows, and the continued failure of Portofino brought a latent demon to the surface.

In mid-March of 2001, the restaurant was not only spiraling downhill, but my third child was just weeks away from being born. On top of that, I couldn't stop drinking after having my first one of the day, usually a glass of wine between nine and ten in the morning. I was ignorant to the concept of alcoholism at that time and baffled as to why I could not stop drinking, especially since the restaurant and my family were so important to me.

Shortly after the birth of my third child, I went to my wife and asked to go into treatment for alcoholism. If I was going to turn

Portofino around, it seemed clear that I was going to have to do it while less drunk than I had been. Timing-wise, I thought I could "spin-dry" for twenty-eight days and be back in time for the busy season. Yes, I know that fellow travelers of sobriety are laughing their asses off about how naïve I was to think my salvation, as well as Portofino's, would be that easy. But every great journey starts with one step, and that moment was my step toward a sober life.

You can guess how excited my wife was when I left her to run a failing restaurant and care for three children ages four, two, and one month old. The shine of my brilliance as a restaurateur and a husband never recovered from that month during which I laid all my burdens on her shoulders.

I returned from treatment mid-May with a renewed spirit for my own well-being and a desire to sink my sober teeth back into Portofino. Having come from treatment, I was convinced that the flaw in my business plan was that I was a drunk, and since that was now fixed, I could focus on being successful. Talk about how stupid is as stupid does!

My month's absence from the business did not aid the improvement of cash flow for Portofino. Quite the opposite—my poor wife had spent most of my absentee month placating vendors and bankers by promising that we would get caught up as soon as the summer season arrived. For over a century, bankers in northwestern Minnesota have been hearing farmers, resort owners, and restaurateurs make that same promise. Though sympathetic, if that crop or those tourist diners don't come in, the bankers do what bankers always do.

During this brief period of sobriety, I was earnestly trying to figure out what was wrong with my restaurant. Why could it not make a profit? I reached out for advice from some of the past owners I had worked for. Funny thing about restaurant owners—the ones who figure out the formula for success are not likely to share it, especially with someone who quit working for them to open their own restaurant. I also reached out to vendors and my CPA for advice. The thing about asking for advice from "industry experts" is that you rarely get any useful business tips, just a whole lot of opinions. Opinions don't equal profits.

Bankers do not know how to run restaurants—they only know how to sell financing products. Architects do not know how to run restaurants—they know how to design and build buildings. CPAs do not know how to run restaurants—they know how to sell tax services. Vendors, even food vendors, do not know how to run restaurants—they know how to sell food products and delivery services. Economics professors do not know restaurants—they know how to research, write, and secure tenure. If you want to learn how to run a restaurant, you have to attach yourself to someone who fought the battles, bears the scars an survived the restaurant business.

I was in desperate need of a business model fix. You see, throughout this painful time, I was hitting my food cost projections, my alcohol cost projections, and the labor cost projections I had modeled in my pro forma. So, I was dumbfounded as to why there wasn't any cash left.

The summer of 2001 opened with a ripple, not the splash required to save Portofino. Our ship listed through the month of June. I kept my sights on July, Independence Day being one of the biggest tourist draws on the Detroit Lakes calendar. The Fourth of July came and went, but July did not fix my cash flow problems. By the third week of July, I no longer had the cash to make payroll. My investor's and my family's funds dried up. There were no more lifeboats, and on a very difficult Sunday night, my wife and I made the decision to shutter the doors on Portofino Restaurant & World Market. The dream of that restaurant, ten years in the making, finally succumbed, and it was a horrible death.

The city leaders who had helped me acquire the land and gave me the variances to build my restaurant were unhappy. My family, who lived in Detroit Lakes, were ashamed. My wife, who had worked alongside me over the last two years to build and operate the restaurant, resented me. My friends, who did their best to support my endeavors, had no idea how to help me. Finding no redeeming features in my own character, I fell off the wagon, hunkered down in my home with a well-stocked wine cabinet and ignored every phone call and letter. And, if all this self-loathing was not bad enough, the realization that I was an alcoholic wrecked any possible enjoyment or relief my old "spirited" friend could offer me.

The next six months were a veritable hell of fending off angry vendors, filing for bankruptcy and trying to keep a positive spin on the home front with three young children. Although it would take six months for the bank to foreclose on the restaurants and bankruptcy protections to kick in, the alcoholic had ample resources to keep his addiction alive. Hundreds of bottles of wine and liquor were in inventory on the day we closed the restaurant's doors.

I'll never forget the last weekend I had the keys to Portofino in early March 2002. I went into the restaurant alone. She had been stripped of just about anything of value that wasn't tied to the mortgage. We had made our final payroll by selling off china, tables, chairs, and whatever inventory still held value. As I walked around the restaurant one last time, the smell of stale grease still lingering in the air, I stood at the bar overlooking a still-frozen Little Detroit Lake. I found a CD player and some old CDs behind the bar. Fumbling through the stack of discs, I came across Eric Clapton's *461 Ocean Boulevard* and popped it into the player.

As Clapton played in the background, I eyed the wine rack behind the bar. About forty dusty bottles of wine remained, mostly inexpensive reds that nobody wanted and I had not consumed. I fumbled behind the bar for a cheap highball glass. All the beautiful Riedel stemware had long since been sold. I popped the cork on a cheap Merlot and walked around the unkept deck of my ship one last time. I guess I was trying to figure out how to say goodbye. I stared out the dining room windows at the frozen, lifeless lake. I walked back toward the kitchen and looked at the idle bread oven, at the beautiful, handcrafted market shelves built to fit perfectly between Palladian windows. I walked by the cold Woodstone pizza oven, with ash still present from the last time it was used. I walked through my kitchen, meticulously designed to serve the "masterpiece" menu

I had created. I wasn't sad, I wasn't happy. Honestly, I think I was just numb. As I walked out of the kitchen and back toward the bar to refill my now empty glass, "Let it Grow" began to play.

> Standing at the crossroads, trying to read the signs
> To tell me which way I should go to find the answer,
> And all the time I know,
> Plant your love and let it grow.
>
> Looking for a reason to check out of my mind,
> Trying hard to get a friend that I can count on,
> But there's nothing left to show,
> Plant your love and let it grow.
>
> Time is getting shorter and there's much for you to do.
> Only ask and you will get what you are needing,
> The rest is up to you.
> Plant your love and let it grow.[2]

The lyrics of the Clapton song caught my attention. "Standing at the crossroads, trying to read the signs. To tell me which way I should go to find the answer…" For whatever reason, this song captivated me on that cold and gray afternoon. I probably hit repeat on the CD player about a dozen times as I continued to drink glass after glass of wine. I would like to say that some great epiphany came to me that weekend as I drank toasts to my soon-to-be-departed restaurant. But what ensued after the closing of Portofino in 2001 was seven years of aimless wandering and alcoholic decline into a self-designed pit of despair.

This book is not about alcoholism, recovery and redemption. If anyone feels a special connection with this part of my story, there is another organization out there full of men and women who are more than eager to talk to you about your terminal uniqueness. My alcoholism is merely part of the story. Alcoholism did not cause my restaurant to fail. It did not cause my marriage to fail. All alcohol did to my life was to put a magnifying glass on my character and all the things I did not know. My alcoholism simply fed the beasts within me, and those beasts were fear and its eternal protector, ego!

At the time I built Portofino, I did know how to write a business plan. I did know how to write a menu. I knew how to design and build a restaurant. I knew how to set up vendor relations. And I knew how to hire and train staff. What I did *not* know how to do was design a profitable business. I could say all the same things about marriage, but this is a book on how to save restaurants, not marriages. Though I suspect if I can teach you how to be a successful restaurateur, you might find it easier to be a successful spouse.

The Quest for Answers

Between 2001 and 2008, I wandered trying to earn a living to support my family and an ever-growing drinking problem. I worked as a general contractor and a home remodeler. I worked as a chef instructor for a culinary school. I worked as a sales manager for a catering company, a sales rep for a Point of Sale (POS) company, a project manager for a real estate development company. I became a restaurant consultant, most notably landing a three-month consulting project on the island of Bermuda. All this time, though, I desperately wanted to know why Portofino had failed, and more importantly, how I could have done it differently. How could I make my next restaurant successful?

Although many of the transient positions I held were in the restaurant or hospitality industry, none of them gave me any clear picture of how to be successful. It is amazing when you think about it how many restaurateurs out there approach their business the way Moses exited Egypt. After some miracle occurs that launches them on their restaurant quest, they spend the next forty years wandering about the desert, listening to everybody around them whine about the poor living conditions and blaming the one Deity who delivered precisely what they wanted in the first place. But I digress…

My real epiphany on how to model a successful restaurant came when I was selling POS systems. It wasn't that these miraculous machines of silicon chips and software code could solve the problem; learning how the restaurant technology interfaces with accounting software started to reveal to me a code for success. You see, up to this point, I had always been a restaurant operator. I ran kitchens, bars, catering operations and entire restaurants. As an operator, I understood what had to occur to hit food costs, labor costs, and other important business performance metrics. What I had never learned was how to set a restaurant up to be profitable in the first place. This is the basic problem with most restaurateurs.

Those of us restaurant types who developed into restaurant operators are taught to manage costs. We are taught that the road to profit means managing every minute detail of the restaurant. If you want to be more profitable, cut your kitchen labor two percent, beat up your vendors, or cut down on your marketing expenses. If you want to be more profitable, get rid of top-end management. For most restaurant operators, more profit comes from trimming expenses.

Don't get me wrong, good business management always includes managing expenses just like a great football team needs a strong defense. That defense may keep your opponent from scoring any points, but you will never win a game unless your offense puts more points on the board than your opponent. Most restaurants that survive the first couple of years have developed a strong defense, but very few put together a winning strategy—a profit-managing strategy. In the next few chapters, I will teach you how to manage profits instead of merely managing expenses.

The Accidental CFO

For those who reading this book for answers on how to run their restaurant more profitably, it is important to ask, *What is the author's pedigree? What makes him some great authority on restaurants?* To this point, I've established that I'm an expert in creating epic failure on both a personal and economic basis. I've also pointed out that I have forty-plus years of restaurant experience, but so did my father. What gives me the authority to talk about the financial operations of the business? I do not have a degree in economics or an MBA. I am not a CPA. I graduated from Hamline University in St. Paul, Minnesota, with a Bachelor of Arts and distinctions in philosophy.

It's not that I didn't try to obtain a business degree. When I entered college as a freshman, I had already been active in the workforce for five years as a manager of a restaurant, developer of menus and wine lists, and as a reasonably accomplished cook. It seemed the logical next move for me was to learn more about business and, more importantly, how to grow successful businesses. I entered my freshman year of college declaring a major in Business Administration. I started the fall semester with macroeconomics and the spring semester with microeconomics. Both those classes, as dull as they usually are, are important foundations to understanding simple and complex economic models.

To earn money for college, a friend and I started a catering company in Detroit Lakes. Our specialty was outdoor barbecues. We converted a two-car garage into a commercial kitchen and custom-designed portable grills and pig roasters to suit our needs. Our motto was *We will bring the party to you!* It was a good and forgiving time to be a young entrepreneur. In the mid-1980s, the economy and summer lake living were booming! So, in the fall of my sophomore year, I signed up for a class entitled "Labor Problems," thinking, *Finally, a class with some practical applications to the restaurant industry.* I was ready to learn as much as I could about building a successful business.

Let me paint a picture of Hamline University's Liberal Arts Economics Department circa 1985. Three academics ran it, two of them well into their sixties. The Economic Department chair was the youngest of the three and around fifty years old. None of these professors had ever stepped foot into an actual business. None had ever signed the front of a payroll check. The closest any of them had come to providing customer service occurred after the university arm-twisting them into being academic advisors. The learned professor who taught the Labor Problems course basically discussed his love of Snickers bars and cigarettes (yes, in 1985 a professor could still light up a heater in the classroom.) His only real claim to fame was writing an academic piece on the unjustness of divorce courts awarding wives a portion of the value of an academic degree if they worked while their spouses pursued doctorates. I think my professor was trying to explain to his newer and younger replacement wife why he had to continue making payments to the previous Mrs. Ph.D.

For a hopeful restaurateur, Labor Problems was a big letdown! For the entire course, when we were not discussing Snickers and cigarettes, we were studying the history of labor versus management disputes. Understanding the history and evolution of labor is, in itself, not an ignoble pursuit, but at Hamline in the mid-80s there were plenty of other courses and academic pursuits that pitted the proletarians against the bourgeoisie. You see, in the restaurants I was associated with, my labor problems were how to keep a cook from grabbing that waitress's ass, how do I get that talented chef to sober up and do his job, and how to teach this high school graduate to make change for a dollar.

If you've seen the Rodney Dangerfield movie *Back to School*, I was basically Thornton Mellon in my Labor Problems class. I wished to discuss real-life labor problems with the professor who presumably had no direct personnel supervision role. After the fall semester of my sophomore year, I vowed never to spend another dime on an economics or business class. To this day, that is a vow I have never broken. Now you know why I ended up with a degree in philosophy. Having determined that learning anything practical at a liberal arts institution was nearly impossible, I switched gears and started learning for learning's sake. I began to learn how to think.

As it turns out, learning how to think versus reciting memorized answers to business situations has served me well. Throughout my career, I developed a knack of absorbing the entirety of the situation and then making a decision based on ethical, legal, and humanistic factors—much to the chagrin of human resource departments that love to spin out volumes of workplace rules. I have learned that putting thinking about a business conundrum in front of the "corporate" rulebook yields faster and more economically satisfactory business decisions.

How the Math Quest Began

The year was 1988, when emerging technology and youth led to my initial understanding of finance. I was in the spring semester of my senior year at Hamline University and writing my senior thesis on Kierkegaard's *Fear and Trembling*. However, in the spring of 1988, my classmates and I did not fear Kierkegaard's confusion about the ontology of God, but rather the looming recession that awaited us upon graduation. I had taken out ten thousand dollars in student loans and was required to pay it back. So, as I desperately crammed for my finals, my business partner—the friend who had started the summer catering business with me—and I got the brilliant idea of opening a restaurant.

There was a dilapidated resort called Dunvilla about twenty miles south of Detroit Lakes, Minnesota. When I say dilapidated, I mean in the strictest sense. In its heyday in the late 1940s and 50s, vacationers stayed in quaint little cabins lined up along the shores of Lake Lizzy, and big bands working the resort circuit played in the sold-out dance hall. Thirty years later, the cabins were falling apart, and the dance hall had been converted to a supper club. Without doing any research whatsoever, my partner and I signed the lease to run the supper club. So, a few months before graduation, not only was I pontificating about Kierkegaard, I was writing a menu and designing a wine list and trying to figure out how to open a restaurant.

Lest you think that right out of college I knew what I was doing, my big strategy for Dunvilla's bold new menu was to go to my nearest competitor, copy most of their menu, and price every offering one dollar less per item. Not unsurprisingly, we became popular. Our little restaurant was only open in the evenings, and after the first month there was a waitlist almost every single evening. I was twenty-two years old and my partner was twenty-one. We were young, stupid, and having lots of fun, although one must question the wisdom of granting a liquor license to a twenty-two-year-old. By and large, though, we survived our own stupidity that first year.

However, when the season came to an end and we added up all the revenue and deducted the expenses, we were left with a big fat goose egg. That was the first time, but not the last, that I had labored my hind end off for no money.

As Dunvilla was only a seasonal restaurant, we shuttered her doors at the end of September. My partner had another year of college to complete, and I returned to the Twin Cities to wait on tables for the winter season (already I had realized serving and bartending made a hell of a lot more money than managing and owning.) Around February, after my partner and I had spent several months licking our wounds, the two of us decided that if we were going to do this restaurant thing for another summer we should figure out how to make it profitable.

We pooled our meager resources and purchased an IBM clone 286 computer. In 1989, this was no small purchase—the cost was north of $2,500. Armed with our shiny new computer, Lotus 1-2-3, and a sincere desire to figure out how to run a successful restaurant, the two of us holed up in a resort hotel in Alexandria, Minnesota, for the long Presidents' Day weekend.

Our strategy session was delayed, however, when we realized our new computer could also play video games, but after growing weary *Jeopardy*, we set to work. The result of that weekend was a custom labor scheduling and payroll tool along with a menu cost program. Though you may be shocked, the strategy of duplicating our competitor's menus at a dollar less per item was not a profitable plan.

There you have it. Back in 1989, the philosophy student, using technology, made his first foray into business analytics. I can guarantee that my old Labor Problems professor was still smoking cigarettes, eating Snickers bars, and trying to figure out why the legal and academic world didn't care that he got hosed in his divorce settlement.

A Series of Fits and Stops

We would go on to run Dunvilla for one more season, and our work on that cold Presidents' Day weekend showed us that a good plan well executed could yield success. We attacked the summer of 1989 armed with the knowledge of what our true food cost was for each menu item as well as the true cost of our weekly payroll. With that, my partner and I were able to establish the proper retail markup to achieve profitability.

At this stage of our young business development, the two of us had to make decisions about what to do with our newfound success. We had entered into the restaurant business partially for the adventure and partially for self-preservation. After our second season of running Dunvilla, we would need to decide a longer-term strategy.

Since the restaurant we leased was part of a dilapidated resort, the banker that held the entire property was uninterested in selling us just the restaurant. I had absolutely no desire to rehabilitate and run an entire resort. If we wanted to grow Dunvilla, we needed a long-term lease or the ability to purchase the property outright. With the restaurant as the only financial hook the banker had to sell that entire property, we were unable to establish anything more than a year-to-year lease. My partner and I decided that it was time to go our separate directions after two seasons. I returned to the Twin Cities to continue my restaurant career.

My resumé of the 1990s became filled with a series of two and three-year positions with various restaurant and catering operations, mostly in the Twin Cities. Within that ten-year span I bought and sold two houses, paid off my student loans, started a family and continued to advance my career in the restaurant industry. With each progressively better job, understanding and integrating technology into the restaurant operation was key to my upward mobility. I became intimately knowledgeable about a wide variety of Restaurant Point of Sale (POS) products as well as product cost control software.

The name of the game in the 90s was integration. That's a fancy word that describes a process of making all the stupid data in one software talk to the stupid data in another software. Integration was sold as some "holy other" bit of technology that, naturally, required expensive integration contracts. The reality was that getting one piece of software to talk to another piece of software means just aligning bits of data in a table and pushing a transfer button. But in the 90s, integration was big business. The cowboys and the smarmy little tech geniuses who understood how to build those tables made a lot of money. It was my job to learn how those tech cowboys created the file transfers so we could take this task in-house and fire the overpriced, Lexus-driving bastards.

I continued to progress from job to job selling my services as a restaurant operational manager with the unique understanding of how to integrate technology into restaurant operations. Quite frankly, that particular role suited me well. I made a decent living, but always lurking in the back of my mind was the desire to own my own restaurant again. In 1998, with a one-year-old child and another on the way, the restaurant bug bit hard. I convinced my wife that it was now or never (or least twenty years from now after the children were grown up). If we were ever going to start a restaurant, this was the time.

There was some logic behind my timing. I was smart enough to realize that waiting a few more years to start a new business venture would be far more difficult with young children in school. I had also grown tired of working for other people. I wanted the freedom that I thought would occur if I was my own boss. I talked about the motivations for why people want to open their own restaurants earlier, but I was really getting tired of working for "idiots." But let me tell you—opening your own restaurant to get away from working for idiots never happens. It merely transfers the image of your stupid boss into the image reflected in the mirror.

Part Three—The Math

"The laws of nature are but the mathematical thoughts of God."

—Euclid of Alexandria

Oh yes, the math. This is usually the part that throws most restaurateurs for a loop. A while back, I was enjoying a nice breakfast with the minister of my church one day when he looked at me somewhat slyly and said, "You know why I got into ministry? There is no math in ministry!"

I have come to understand that a lot of people get into the restaurant business under the same notion. I mean, when you think about the people you know in the restaurant business, they are by and large the academic nonconformists. You can spot a future restaurateur in elementary school. They are the ones with "doesn't play well with others" checked on their report cards. Future restaurateurs are the young charges in school who struggle sitting still in their seats, standing patiently in line, and focusing on the task at hand. Future restaurateurs stare out the classroom window dreaming about what life will be like when they are released from their academic prison. They often fall asleep during math class or prefer to doodle in the margins of their homework rather than work through mathematical equations.

Fortunately for my industry, restaurants are the perfect landing spot for all the young "academics" who did not pay attention to the teacher and the chalkboard. The hospitality industry is fat with the ones who struggled with paying attention to the task at hand and stared out the window, the individuals who dreamed of cutting the chains that held them to their desk and instead dreamed of adventure. Where most academic and corporate settings require employees who can stay focused on a single task, the carnival we call a restaurant actually requires staff that can multitask and thrive on unpredictability. This industry is one of the places where people diagnosed with ADD truly succeed. But it would take another book to cover how academia fails to address these unique characteristics and nurture these future "single task" nonconformists.

All that said, you now know why the restaurant industry is not filled with STEM and economic majors. To be honest, those who may understand the math behind creating successful restaurants—CPAs, MBAs and architects—don't have the stomach or the will to work the required hours to run a successful restaurant. I have tried in vain to explain to my CPA how I could have a negative balance in my checkbook on Friday but still cover my payroll on Monday. I have talked to purchasing managers who tried to convince me that switching from 2% to1% mozzarella cheese would save me thousands of dollars per month, who could not understand how a drop in the quality of our food would cost me way more than the fifteen-cent per pound savings. Attorneys are quite useful at putting the language and protection together for contracts, but God help you if you rely on them for financial advice for your restaurant. People in the business of protecting you from liability have no business consulting with you on owning your own restaurant because you, the budding restaurateur, are basically throwing all caution to the wind and venturing into a place where security is a rarity.

The reality is, if you want to know the components for a successful restaurant, it takes a fair amount of all three Ms. Successful restaurateurs need a healthy dose but tempered application of the myths, a knack for creating the magic, and an understanding of how to mathematically position your restaurant for success. The trick to becoming a successful restaurant entrepreneur is to manage the healthy balance between all three. Too much myth and no math and your restaurant fails. Too much magic and no myth, and your restaurant fails. Too much math and no myths or magic and your restaurant fails. For those of you thinking of entering the restaurant business, or if you're already there, and you find that you are lacking in one of these key areas, I advise you to find a partner or hire an individual who can supply that deficiency.

Figuring out the math required to make a restaurant profitable is where many independent restaurateurs run into trouble. Opinions and methods vary widely as to how one should go about modeling a restaurant for profit. Again, in most cases, revenue for restaurants is derived by establishing a retail price for commodities listed on a menu of options. Establishing the proper markup in an industry that makes pennies per item makes or breaks every restaurant. Standard industry practices for pricing a menu generally fall into the following three categories:

1. See what the competitors are charging and charge a little more or a little less. Or, change plate presentational portion sizes so they are not comparable to the competition.
2. Determine the food cost percentage needed for desired profit and multiply each cost by that percent.
3. Attempt to determine the actual cost involved in preparing and serving each item, including overhead and profit, and add this to the food cost to determine the final price for each menu item. (Make a standard gross profit on each item.) From a practical point of view, this method is most difficult.[3]

Because method 3 is the most difficult to produce, most independent restaurants employ method 1 or 2 (or a hybrid of both.)

Method 1 was my "Dunvilla" approach toward pricing my first menu. The major problem with using this method is that it does not account for sales volume, and overhead as a percent of that volume. Generally, the higher the sales revenue, the lower the overhead as a percent of that volume. A restaurant producing two million per year in revenue can absorb overhead more efficiently than a restaurant hovering at one million a year. Not taking overhead as a percent to total revenue can prove disastrous if a restaurant is merely pricing menus in accordance with competitors. This is why my first season at Dunvilla was unsuccessful. I not only copied my nearest competitor's menu and charged a dollar less per item, but I made that brilliant move with a restaurant that produced half of my competitor's annual sales volume.

Method 2 is slightly better, but only if you can determine the correct food cost percentage to yield the desired profit. Method 2 is what I used when determining the retail prices for my restaurant Portofino. The danger here is in setting up a desired food cost percentage and managing to that percentage without knowing *whether that is the correct percentage* to produce the desired profit.

Here, one must look at the whole financial picture and determine overhead as a percent to sales in order to reach an accurate food cost percentage for profit. Simply relying on industry standards for food cost percentages carries the same problem as my example in Method 1. A restaurant producing two million in annual revenue still has a lower overhead percentage to revenue than a restaurant producing one million.

In a sense, setting your food cost percentage to industry standards basically establishes a business model that only works when revenue meets or exceeds the artificial food cost percentage targeted. This is what I refer to as the "sweet spot" method. There is a spot in all restaurant models whereby a predetermined food cost percentage intersects with sales revenue that produces the desired profit. But if the sales revenue never reaches that "sweet spot," or if it fluctuates, such as in seasonal businesses, merely modeling a restaurant on a predetermined food cost percentage may prove disastrous.

As noted above, method 3 is the most difficult to execute. But establishing a gross profit on each menu item is the only way to design retail pricing on menus to make certain you meet your desired profitability. Utilizing method 3 allows every restaurateur to determine precisely what his or her menu pricing should be in order to make a profit *regardless of annual sales volume*.

Since profit is the goal of rational restaurant owners, it is important to spend some time reviewing the mathematics involved in producing that desire. Simple enough. Here is the equation for determining profit:

P (Profit) = R (Revenue) – E (Expenses)

The equation above is true for understanding profit as well as loss. Spend less on food, labor, and overhead than total revenue and the business makes a profit. Spend more on expenses than revenue, and the business loses money. So, if one wants to increase P, they must increase R or reduce E (or a combination of both). Honestly, this is the internal bogeyman for all independent restaurant operators—the nagging apprehension that keeps them awake at night. And I must say, far too many restaurateurs think the revenue portion of this equation is the Holy Grail solution to their financial problems.

However, what happens if increasing R results in increasing E? This approach to managing profit is what I previously referred to as the dartboard method—you keep lobbing darts at the board hoping you can increase R enough to overcome the increasing E. For example, consider the discounting dilemma. BOGO (Buy One Get One) promotions come to mind. The BOGO may increase R, but it also increases E.

Another target on the dartboard is the "lost leader" menu items—happy hour discounts of popular signature items sold at steep discounts. The loss leader strategy sells an item at a loss and hopes the customer also orders enough profitable items to overcome the loss. This "make it up in volume" approach only works if the menu mix distribution of high-profit high-volume items is greater than no- or low-profit items.

There is a better way to establish retail markup that ensures desired profitability for every restaurant.

I Had to Figure Out Accounting

It was 2008, and I'd finally determined to give real sobriety a chance. I had been a restaurant operator living the hard-drinking life of a restaurant operator. I worked the long hours, nights, and weekends that were required to be a great restaurant operator. But, I determined, if I was to give sobriety, saving my marriage and fatherhood a chance, I needed to make a change. No longer could I be the guy who worked sixty to seventy hours a week, closing down the restaurants and performing "quality checks" on my bartenders' most recent concoctions. I was going to need a "day job." If I was to stay in the same industry, I would have to become one of those dreaded "corporate stiffs." You know the type—the number crunchers and rule makers who sit in their cushy offices all day. They are the ones who bring a table of four into the restaurant to dine at the busiest time of the day, the ones who call the restaurant in the middle of the lunch rush to convey some useless and pointless dictate about how to run a restaurant. Yes, if I were to make the changes necessary in my life to survive, I had to become that guy.

At this stage of restaurant technology, restaurants were in real need of integrating data gathered by the POS into business analytical software as well as accounting software. It was also at this time that I started developing a true understanding of how math could solve the profit dilemmas that previously eluded me.

First off, since I was selling myself as someone who could integrate POS data into accounting software packages, I had to learn what the hell accounting software actually did with the numbers. Double entry accounting, debits and credits, expense versus capital accounts and net profit versus retained earnings are just a few concepts I had to learn to do the job of data integration. The reality is, accounting math rarely extends beyond the basic concepts of addition, subtraction, multiplication and division. If my math teachers would've convinced me these concepts were useful to putting money in my pocket and growing wealth, I may have paid more attention in class. I can, however, report that after thirty years of running businesses, I have never needed to calculate the distance two trains covered after leaving the station traveling in opposite directions at thirty and sixty miles per hour respectively. At least for me, it was far more fun using math to do my job when I could see tangible results.

Something unusual happened once I truly started digging into the accounting of restaurants. Those little black and red digits in debit and credit columns started to speak to me. I started seeing mathematical patterns.

Sales - Cost of Goods Sold (COGS) - labor = Gross Profit

Gross Profit - Expenses = Net Operating Profit

Net Operating Profit - Non-Controllable Overhead = Net Income

All those little numbers on the screens represented percentages of the whole. Positive Net Income percentages meant profit. Negative Net Income percentages meant loss. Despite what my football coach used to say when he told the team that we need to give 110 percent effort, the notion of making a profit relies on the fact that 100 percent is the total revenue and the difference between profit and loss is how the percentages are managed from 100 percent revenue.

Understanding how a profit and loss statement operates helped me figure out profitability but didn't necessarily teach me what the key independent expenses—like food, alcohol and labor—should be. However, after studying multiple restaurant Profit & Loss statements, I started to see restaurant operations as a mathematical equation—a formulaic method that could help predict and achieve desired profit. To be honest, most independent restaurants use the "dartboard" method to set the key target percentages of food and liquor costs.

The dartboard approach is the method of looking at an income statement and individually tweaking expense line items until a magical theoretical profit can be projected. Don't get me wrong, I worked for some very successful restaurateurs who have mastered the method of throwing darts at the expense percentages on their income statements. I once worked for a guy who literally sold over ten thousand items. We laid those items out in a spreadsheet and manually tweaked the retail price we thought we could get and then let the spreadsheet roll up a theoretical profit into our model. If we didn't like the results, we went through the ten thousand items and adjusted again. It was slow, tedious, and we did it twice a year. But it worked, and that restaurant continues to be successful to this day.

I have worked for restaurant owners who still use the "Dunvilla" profit-modeling approach. They take the temperature of the market and their competitors' menu pricing, then set their retail prices accordingly. To make this pricing strategy work, the restaurant owner then sets to work managing the expenses down to the point where the restaurant makes a profit. Like my first year at Dunvilla, this method proved quite successful at bringing customers through my door. But if your sales volume is not substantially higher or your overhead lower, this is a method guaranteed to lose money.

I have worked for restaurant owners who first set their food cost percentage to their desired level and then worked to bring the expenses in line in order to make a profit. That was my method at Portofino. However, as with Portofino and Dunvilla, these two methods can also prove fatal, especially if projected revenues fall short!

What I learned, unfortunately too late in my life to save my dream restaurant was that there was a foolproof mathematical equation for establishing retail pricing structures and subsequent COGS percentage targets. If you set your retail pricing structure correctly, you can manage profitability instead of managing expenses.

You want to talk about disrupting the entire industry? Teaching independent restaurateurs how to set their retail prices for profit is a game changer. Don't get me wrong—at no time am I advocating ignoring the importance of managing expenses. But if the restaurant business model is not designed to produce a profit, managing expenses may just serve the purpose of mitigating losses.

What Is the Right Food Cost Percentage?

Indeed, what *is* the right food cost percentage a restaurant should target? Most restaurant owners first set their retail menu prices, then attempt to manage their expenses in the hopes of making a profit. This method perpetuates the myth that there is a correct industry standard food cost percentage and labor cost percentage that, if hit, will make the business successful.

Put me in front of a hundred restaurant operators, and I would get a hundred different answers to the question, "What is the right food cost percentage?" I would see answers ranging from 24 percent of food sales all the way up to 38 percent. And, depending on the type of operation and overhead, every one of those answers may be right.

However, the real question every operator should ask is this—to what percentage do you need to set your food costs in order to make a 10 percent bottom-line profit? Or a 12 percent bottom-line profit? Or a 20 percent bottom-line profit?

If the guy running a 30 percent food cost is hitting a 10 percent bottom-line profit, the answer is pretty simple—the proper food cost percentage is 30 percent. But if Mr. 30 Percent is only producing a 6 percent profit, what should his food cost be in order to bring bottom-line profit up four percentage points? Here is where I usually lose most of the restaurateurs, because they look at me and say, "In order to make a 10 percent bottom-line profit, I need to run a 26 percent food cost?"

No!

But to get there, we have to do some math.

The Overhead Conundrum

Figuring out overhead, it turns out, was the missing piece of the puzzle that eluded me in my early years of restaurant development.

I did not learn this lesson until I took a position with a company that had a wide variety of revenue models and leasehold contracts. This group had several polished-casual concepts, a seafood restaurant, and several pizza shops. The annual revenue per store ranged from six hundred thousand to six million dollars.

When I came on board with that company, all five concepts were designed to hit the same food costs, liquor costs and labor costs. Not surprisingly, the six-million-dollar restaurant threw off a lot more profit than the six-hundred-thousand-dollar one, both in real dollars and as a percent to revenue. It was as financial controller of this small restaurant group that I learned the importance of understanding overhead.

For the purposes of this discussion, overhead refers to labor, benefits, direct, fixed and corporate expenses. Fixed and corporate expenses are line items like rent, business insurance, interest on all debt repayments, and depreciation. In my experience above, those overhead percentages ranged from 8 to 18 percent.

As it turned out, understanding the relationship of overhead as it relates to Cost of Goods Sold is the most important factor in understanding how to set profitable restaurant business models. For me, this is when my job as a CFO got exciting. No longer was I merely the historian of our businesses, reporting the good or bad results of our operations. I became a positive source for improving profitability within our group.

So, let's get to the math.

The Importance of Understanding Overhead

A restaurateur who wishes to manage their profit must first understand how to calculate the breakeven point of his business. The following statement is quite controversial within my own community, but it needs to be said, because far too many restaurateurs are chasing the wrong solutions to their profit woes:

Food costs and labor costs are not the reason restaurants are unprofitable!

Taking this a step further, restaurant owners who spend most of their time trying to mitigate these two key expense categories will more than likely damage their business rather than solve their profit problem. If cutting food costs means dropping food quality, the customer will notice the diminished quality and move on. If scaling back labor is a means to dropping labor costs, the customer will notice the diminished service and move on.

In my forty-plus years of restaurant operations, I have found the number one problem hindering profit at every restaurant was not the cost of raw product or the cost of labor. It was understanding how to price their menu to accommodate the necessary raw costs, labor and overhead required to meet the concept's objective.

If you wish to design a restaurant that makes a profit, you first must learn how to cost out menus and apply the right markup. Again, it is important to understand that restaurants are not just selling food and alcohol. Restaurants, bars, nightclubs, catering facilities, even coffee shops are selling *experiences*.

How do you put a price tag on an experience? Quite simply, restaurants price out the experience on their menu. Everyone knows you can buy whole bean coffee, grind it up at home, and brew a pot of coffee for less money than standing in line at your favorite coffee shop for your daily cup of Joe. The price that coffee shop charges for a grande mocha cappuccino covers the cost to break even for the expense of providing the experience and also returns a profit to the owners. The sooner restaurant owners understand that their retail menu prices must cover the cost for providing the five-sensory experience of hearing, sight, touch, taste and smell, the better they will become at making a profit. Because when restaurant owners understand how to set their menu pricing to return their desired profit, the model will dictate the targeted food cost percentage, targeted alcohol cost percentage, and labor percentages to manage.

In my experience, profitable restaurant owners are much happier and sleep much better at night.

This is the greatest challenge for independent restaurateurs—trying to work out what a customer will spend on a beautifully grilled piece of salmon or a marbled and perfectly aged ribeye steak based on their perceived value.

Don't get me wrong, there is an acceptable range that a reasonable customer will pay for both items, but what a successful restaurateur needs to ask himself is this: "What will my customers pay for the experience? What will my customers pay for a beautifully appointed restaurant with lighting that makes my date look even more attractive, for a polished server who makes the customer look smarter by suggesting the perfect bottle of wine, for a chef who knows exactly how long to perfectly grill a piece of fish, for a pastry chef who spent all afternoon crafting the perfect tiramisu, and for the personal touch of the manager or owner who comes over to my table and personally thanks me for choosing their restaurant?"

Restaurants run tight margins—it's a game of pennies. Making a profit is cobbling enough pennies together at the end of each week. So, if profit is a game of pennies, why do independent restaurant owners spend so little time figuring out how many pennies over breakeven they should charge?

The key to this is learning how to find the breakeven point for each restaurant. Every business has one. Once breakeven can be established, designing a menu for profit is a simple exercise of calculating the retail price of your menu that exceeds breakeven. It's fairly simple to do. All one needs is a Profit and Loss Statement and a calculator.

Breakeven is the point where Revenue less COGS less Expenses equals zero, or:

(R – COGS – E = 0)

Finding the overall breakpoint of a restaurant is relatively easy, but how do you find the breakeven point on each menu item? This breakeven number is the raw cost of the item, and that menu item's share of labor, variable, fixed and corporate expenses. To find the breakeven point on every individual menu item, we do need to perform a little bit of math.

First, we must establish what the *overhead factor* (OHF) is for the entire restaurant. To do this, we must calculate the *ratio of expenses* compared to the *raw product* costs of the restaurant. For this exercise, we'll have to review the current income statement. Establishing the ratio of labor, variable, fixed and corporate expenses to the raw product cost helps us determine the precise breakeven dollar amount for each menu item.

Starting with the Income Statement (or Profit & Loss Statement,) highlight the total Cost of Goods Sold (COGS) and the totals for labor, variable, fixed, and corporate expenses. Then, to determine the overhead factor, use the following formula:

COGS / (Labor + Variable + Fixed + Corporate) = OHF

For example:
1,085,031 / (1,259,385 + 365,639 + 142249 + 279,623) = 1.89

Profit & Loss Statement

	M3	
Total Sales	**3,245,666**	100.00%
Prime Cost		
Food and Alcohol Costs (COGS)	1,085,031	33.43%
Labor and Benefits	1,259,385	38.80%
Total Prime Cost	**2,344,416**	72.23%
Gross Profit	**901,250**	27.77%
Operating Expense		
G&A	105,019	3.24%
Direct Operating Expenses	154,075	4.75%
Repair and Maintenance	30,611	0.94%
Utilities	9,057	0.28%
Marketing/Promotions	66,877	2.06%
Total Operating Expense	**365,639**	11.27%
Net Operating Income	**535,611**	16.50%
Non Controllable Expense		
Fixed Expenses	142,249	4.38%
Total Corporate Overhead & Other	**279,623**	8.62%
Net Profit	**113,739**	3.50%

The Overhead Factor is 1.89

The next step is to determine what the breakeven (BE) number is for any individual menu item. To do this, you take the Raw Product Cost (RPC) multiplied by the Overhead Factor (OHF) plus RPC:

(RPC x OHF) + RPC = BE

For simplicity sake, let's assume the raw product cost of a cappuccino is $1.00. The breakeven formula looks like this:

(1.00 x 1.89) + 1.00 = 2.89

For our theoretical restaurant, the breakeven point on our cappuccino costing one dollar is $2.89. If the retail price is below $2.89, selling this item represents a *real loss* and every penny over $2.89 represents a *real profit*.

Now, if your goal is a 10 percent bottom-line profit, the math required to establish retail price is relatively simple. We now know the breakeven point for our cappuccino is $2.89. To calculate the retail markup necessary to achieve a 10 percent bottom-line profit, we simply need to divide our breakeven number (BE) by the reciprocal of the desired profit. To find the reciprocal for this example, you subtract the percent of desired profit from 100%:

100% - 10% = 90% (1.00 - .10 = .90)

For instance, if the restaurant desires a 10 percent profit, we divide by the reciprocal or 0.9. If the desire is for a 15 percent profit, we divide by 0.85, and so on.

Let's go back to our example. Our cappuccino with a $1.00 raw product cost has a breakeven value of $2.89. To determine the retail markup ensuring a 10 percent profit, we divide $2.89 by 0.9, giving us the proper price of $3.21. Personally, I would round the retail price up to $3.25.

BE/reciprocal of profit percent = markup

$2.89 / 0.9 = $3.21

Now, what is the proper COGS percentage is for the whole restaurant in order to ensure they achieve a 10 percent profit? Again, this is simple math. We divide our raw cost of $1.00 by our markup price of $3.25.

RPC / Retail = COGS %

$1.00 / $3.21 = 31.1%

Let's run this again for a more complex menu item, a fresh salmon entrée with a chili pepper sauce. An 8-ounce salmon filet is $7.10, and the sauce is another $0.25, giving us a raw product cost of $7.35. First, we establish the breakeven amount by applying the formula:

(7.35 x 1.89) + 7.35 = 21.24

The breakeven point for the salmon filet with chili pepper sauce is $21.24. To establish the proper retail markup for this item ensuring a 10 percent profit, we simply divide by the reciprocal of 10 percent or 0.9.

$21.24 / 0.9 = $23.60

Thus, the proper retail markup for our salmon filet is $23.60. Again, if we divide the raw product cost by the retail markup, we will get the targeted food cost percentage of 31.1 percent. This pricing method should be applied to every item on a restaurant menu.

$7.35 / $23.60 = 31.1%

But, you say, I can get $25 for that salmon, giving me the lower food cost percentage of 29.4 percent. Maybe, but what about your 20-ounce bone-in ribeye that costs $17.50? Are you setting that menu item up for success? Let's run the ribeye through the formula gauntlet.

(17.50 x 1.89) + 17.50 = 50.57

50.57 / 0.9 = 56.20

17.50 / 56.20 = 31.1%

The price required to achieve a 10 percent profit is $56.20, or 31.1 percent COGS. If I were setting the retail menu prices on the grilled salmon with red chilis sauce and the bone in ribeye, the menu prices would be $24 and $56 respectively. I know selling both those items will achieve my profitability cost of goods goal of roughly 31 percent.

There are some restaurant operators who like to play the "menu mix lottery" when pricing out their menus. These operators would charge more for the salmon because the market would bear a higher price and less for the ribeye, especially if they had a strategy where they did not want to price anything on the menu over $49. I call this the "menu mix lottery" because now the operator hopes they sell more salmon at a lower food cost percentage then ribeyes. If the reverse happens and the beef far outsells the fish—which is typical with seasonality of customer preferences—the operator will experience a higher overall food cost.

For an example of how to use the overhead calculation method for establishing proper retail markups, I've highlighted the relevant totals on three separate Profit & Loss statements below to show you how different restaurant establishments have different overhead costs.

Profit & Loss Statement

	M1		M2		M3	
Total Sales	**6,962,090**	100.00%	**3,694,392**	100.00%	**3,245,666**	100.00%
Prime Cost						
Food and Alcohol Costs (COGS)	2,079,915	29.87%	1,149,520	31.12%	1,085,031	33.43%
Labor and Benefits	2,533,473	36.39%	1,453,650	39.35%	1,259,385	38.80%
Total Prime Cost	**4,613,388**	66.26%	**2,603,170**	70.46%	**2,344,416**	72.23%
Gross Profit	**2,348,703**	33.74%	**1,091,222**	29.54%	**901,250**	27.77%
Operating Expense						
G&A	205,922	2.96%	112,785	3.05%	105,019	3.24%
Direct Operating Expenses	307,761	4.42%	184,632	5.00%	154,075	4.75%
Repair and Maintenance	46,542	0.67%	57,234	1.55%	30,611	0.94%
Utilities	106,581	1.53%	96,672	2.62%	9,057	0.28%
Marketing/Promotions	115,429	1.66%	92,178	2.50%	66,877	2.06%
Total Operating Expense	**782,235**	11.24%	**543,501**	14.71%	**365,639**	11.27%
Net Operating Income	**1,566,468**	22.50%	**547,721**	14.83%	**535,611**	16.50%
Non Controllable Expense						
Fixed Expenses	387,867	5.57%	225,744	6.11%	142,249	4.38%
Total Corporate Overhead & Other	**603,078**	8.66%	**329,744**	8.93%	**279,623**	8.62%
Net Profit	**575,523**	8.27%	**-7,766**	-0.21%	**113,739**	3.50%

How to Find Break Even:

Step #1 **Calculate the Overhead Factor OHF =COGS/ Total Expenses**

COGS	2,079,915	1,149,520	1,085,031
Total Expenses	4,306,653	2,552,639	2,046,896
Overhead Factor	2.07	2.22	1.89

Step #2 **Calculate Breakeven Raw Product (RP) Cost X OHF + RP**

Break Even Cost (raw Product cost = $1.00)	3.07	3.22	2.89

Step #3 **Calculate Retail Mark up based on desired Profit % BEC / reciprocal of desired profit**

Example at 10% profit (BEC/.9)	**$3.41**	**$3.58**	**$3.21**

As you can see, determining the proper markup to ensure profitability is essential. For the three examples above, for every $1.00 of raw product cost, M1 has a breakeven point of $3.07, M2 has a breakeven point of $3.22, and M3 has a breakeven point of $2.89. So, if the M3 pricing model is used at the M2 restaurant, they will lose money on each transaction—exactly one penny. But making a profit in the restaurant business is all about managing the pennies!

Now, say you're trying to price a cappuccino for all three restaurants. To ensure a 10 percent bottom-line profit, M1 must sell it for at least $3.41. M2 must get $3.58. However, M3 could sell it for $3.25 and easily clear the 10 percent profit hurdle.

It's hard to imagine, but as a CFO the greatest challenge I have is explaining this mathematical pricing model to restaurant owners. For starters, fear usually kicks in when they're confronted with the reality that pricing a cappuccino for $3.00 across all three stores can't possibly meet the same profit expectation. The reason is that the raw cost percentages are the same in all three cases, but the *overhead* is different for each. A $3.00 dollar cappuccino sold at M1 and M2 loses $0.07 and $0.22 respectively.

Ten years ago, I was working for a restaurant group as a consultant to help identify a cash flow problem. One of the restaurants in this group sold an appetizer called Tenderloin Bleu Cheese Fondue. This item had about six ounces of tenderloin tips sautéed in an herb butter, served with cubed bread and a warm bleu cheese fondue dipping sauce. It was quite yummy! The retail price on this item was $12.95. After costing out this item and applying the overhead factor, the breakeven point was $13. To make a 10 percent profit, this restaurant would need to charge $14.45.

The ownership pulled the "loss leader" argument that people who came in for this popular item would order other menu items—undoubtably true. Grocery stores discount turkeys at Thanksgiving so they can sell very profitable potatoes, sage, allspice and cranberries. But here comes the kicker—this Tenderloin Bleu Cheese Fondue was available for happy hour at $9.95!

It turns out that most of the dish's sales were between the hours of four and six o'clock. So now, not only were they not breaking even, they were losing three dollars every time it left the kitchen at happy hour. On top of that, because of its popularity, they no longer used just the tenderloin tip scraps. They were chopping up whole tenderloins just to meet the demand.

Again, the ownership was steadfast that this item drove customers to the restaurant. My response was, of course it would! Where can I get 6 ounces of beef tenderloin for $10? Hell, I could order two of them with two of your happy hour beers and I'd have 12 ounces of tenderloin and a couple of drinks for $25.

I convinced them to drop the item when I reached into my pocket and pulled out a fistful of dollar bills and threw them on the table. I said, "Here is your new marketing strategy. For every customer who wants to order that tenderloin at happy hour, instruct your servers to peel out two one-dollar bills and say, 'I will pay you two dollars to order anything else on the menu.'" That establishment literally was losing three dollars every time Beef Tenderloin went out for happy hour.

Now that I've explained how to set the retail price in order to ensure you hit your desired profitability, the next step is to establish what your true Cost of Goods percentages ought to be in these three scenarios. M1 should be selling its cappuccino for $3.45, yielding a product cost percentage of 29 percent, and M2 should be selling cappuccino for $3.60 at 28 percent. Finally, M3 should be selling the cappuccino for $3.25, at 31 percent. Just like the retail prices, the actual cost of goods percentage varies in all three of these restaurants based on their individual overhead requirements.

What about Alcohol?

Until now, I have been assuming that my mythical restaurants are selling food only. How do we handle restaurant concepts that sell both food and alcohol? Most restaurants run far lower cost of goods percentages on their alcohol sales, but bar programs vary based on the concept. Nightclubs have different retail target costs per drink than your neighborhood local. Restaurant concepts with extensive wine lists have different cost percentage targets than casual-service restaurants. But the pricing concept is the same.

If your goal is to make 10 percent profit and you're able to yield a 24 percent cost of goods on alcohol items, we need merely to understand what percent of your sales of alcohol versus food are and adjust the target percentages accordingly. The math here gets a little more complicated, but the same scenario for retail pricing is in play.

To find proper Cost of Goods percentages for both food and alcohol we need to have one known variable. In this case, we know that alcohol costs are 24 percent. If our sales splits are 75 percent food and 25 percent alcohol, we know through our prior exercise that to make our 10 percent profit, our *overall* targeted Cost of Goods is 31 percent. Calculating the target food cost percentage is just a matter of filling in the unknown allocated dollars for food costs. Take a look at this example.

Sales Splits:		
Food Sales	$2,434,249	75%
Alcohol Sales	$ 811,416	25%
Target COGS	**$1,011,991**	**31%**
Food Costs	$ 817,251	34%
Alcohol Costs	$ 194,740	24%

In the example above, we know that alcohol costs are $194,740, or 24 percent of alcohol sales. We also know through our previous calculations that the target COGS for this restaurant to make 10 percent profit is 31 percent. All we need to do is calculate the remaining dollars allocated to food costs and then divide that by food sales. For the example below, targeted COGS at 31 percent equals $1,011,991. Subtract the known alcohol cost quantity of $194,740 at the 24 percent COGS from $1,011,991 and we get a remaining balance of $817,251. To get the acceptable food cost percentage of 34 percent, divide $817,251 by the total food sales of $2,434,249.

You've seen how mere pennies can be the difference between making money and losing it. This is why Portofino failed even though I was hitting my artificial target cost of goods percentages and labor costs percentages—I didn't how to calculate my overhead and price my menu accordingly. When my restaurant was failing, I was throwing out lifelines to friends, restaurant owners, CPAs and bankers asking for help. If they knew my problem was that my menu wasn't priced for profit based on my overhead, they surely kept that to themselves. I'm writing this book as a lifeline to all those entrepreneurial dreamers who want to open a restaurant of their own, or perhaps already have, and now find themselves on the perpetual hamster wheel running like crazy but going nowhere.

Learning how to price your menu is not complicated and does not take expensive and time-consuming software, although there are some great and affordable technologies now available. Everything I have explained can be achieved as long as the restaurant has an accurate Income Statement, a pad of paper, a pencil and a calculator. But the independent restaurateur must know the raw product cost of *everything they sell*. Henry Ford didn't sell a car without knowing its cost. Big-box retailers don't sell a single product without knowing its cost. Chain restaurants don't sell products without knowing their costs. And you, the independent restaurant owner, cannot write a menu without knowing what each item costs.

My final note on using overhead as a factor in creating profitable menu pricing has to do with managing expenses. As you can see in my calculations, the expenses that fed overhead were labor, direct operating expenses, occupancy expenses, interest on debt, etc. Just because I revealed a retail pricing method for ensuring that you price your menu for profit doesn't mean you ignore those other expenses. The more you can lower overhead, the greater the percent of profit you could realistically achieve within your market—maybe even pushing for 12 or 15 percent profit.

More importantly, the more you can manage your expenses, the better you can compete with other restaurants. There is great comfort in knowing that you can set your menu prices at or below your competitor's prices and still make your profit goals. It is comforting to know that you can out-compete a national brand because your overhead and profit needs are lower. You never know, maybe some young know-it-all graduate with a four-year B.A. degree will open a restaurant next to yours and attempt to put you out of business by duplicating your menu and charging a dollar less for each item.

You will not need to conduct the elaborate scheme of driving your new competitor out of business, as was the fate of Chef Primo in the classic movie *The Big Night*. You simply need to let time run its course on your competitor's business. Because unless they are paying substantially less for labor, food, rent and debt service, their model of selling menu items for one dollar less will seal their fate just the same as it did mine at Dunvilla and Portofino.

Financial Setup for Success

In order to establish your true overhead costs, you must produce accurate financial statements. This is an area where most first-time restaurant owners fall flat. Remember, a great many creative and talented chefs and restaurant operators are driven to the restaurant industry because they enjoy creating the environments that stimulate the five senses. Certainly, good restaurant operators need to focus on those five senses to create and maintain the magic of their restaurants.

Most first-time operators, however, fail to see the importance of establishing solid and accurate accounting of their operations. To be honest, running restaurants requires dealing with the here and now of daily business. Accounting falls into the realm of tomorrow. It is imperative that restaurateurs invest in the personnel and technology to manage the daily financial aspects of their businesses.

When I look back at the epic failure that was Portofino, producing timely and accurate Profit & Loss statements was one of my biggest oversights. I was so focused on the day-to-day operations (and survival) of my restaurant, I ignored the absolute need to hire someone to keep the day-to-day financial bookkeeping up to date. *New restaurant business plans must include the cost to maintain daily financial information*, whether those costs are derived by a third-party provider, an on-staff bookkeeper, innovative technology, or a combination of all three. It is just as crucial to restaurant business success to have a well-maintained financial machine as it is to have well-serviced kitchen equipment. The failure of either of these will spell disaster for the new restaurateur.

At a minimum, a financial statement needs to show Revenue, COGS, Labor, Controllable Expenses and Non-Controllable Expenses. I prefer a greater breakdown as shown in the Appendix at the end of this book. This allows for greater understanding of the business.

A detailed financial statement is useful for the second most important aspect of running a restaurant—creating a budget. I cannot emphasize enough the importance of establishing monthly and annual budgets for your business. Far too many restaurateurs ignore this crucial aspect of running their businesses. You must take the time to project your expectations and measure your success at achieving those goals on a month-to-month basis.

The Economics of Political Decisions

As a restaurant CFO, I cannot ignore discussing how politics, regulation and ever-changing economic factors affect the hospitality industry. There are now three certainties in life—death, taxes and regulatory manipulation for political gain. My mathematical equations cannot help with the first two certainties, but it will help with the third.

Whether a business owner is for or against an increase in minimum wage, mandatory plastic bans and employer-sponsored health care, he or she must know how to price their menu to accommodate for the added expenses that these policies create. Understanding how to reprice restaurant menus to absorb the additional overhead created by regulatory legislation is an essential skill all restaurateurs need in our politically manipulated twenty-first century economic landscape.

Interestingly, my experience has shown that restaurant operators who support certain regulatory mandates such as higher minimum wage or employee sponsored health care are far more proactive at adjusting the retail pricing structure to absorb the expenses than those business owners who disagree with the policies. Some restaurant owners ignore particular policies they disagree with believing that the economic impact of that policy will simply go away. Believe me, it doesn't.

Here's the rub. Regardless of political affiliations, there are two competing regulatory realities facing restaurants. First, restaurants face a plethora of design and operational regulations demanded by a multitude of local, state and federal agencies. These zoning requirements include multitudes of taxing requirements, ACA requirements, health code requirements and recycling requirements to name a few.

Secondly, businesses are charged to regulate a wide variety of social dictates such as antidiscrimination, gender equality and family leave/personal time off requirements. In a sense, what all levels of government create is a set of preferred living requirements for its citizens to abide by. But the reality is that governments have limited power in forcing individual citizens to act in accordance with their regulatory desires. The real power in government enacting policies for societal evolution comes not from forcing direct adherence from the people themselves but by demanding businesses to play the "enforcer" of enacted policy.

Since businesses are required to ask government for permission to operate through licensing, permitting and taxing processes, governments have the power to demand from businesses that which they could never command from their citizens. Budding restaurateurs may think they want to open a restaurant because they love serving great food and drinks, but they also must know that they will be required to be a therapist, healthcare expert, building code wonk, insurance professional and employment law guru. Each of these added burdens on business owners have real costs associated with them, and business owners must learn how to capture them in the retail pricing strategy.

In fact, government covertly demands that they be profitable. This was made especially clear in the Dodd-Frank banking regulations of 2009. You see, after the housing meltdown of 2008, Congress became quite upset that lending institutions were not following conservative lending principles such as selling commercial loans only to businesses capable of repaying them. So, with the heat turned up on commercial lenders to lend money only to businesses that make a profit, Dodd-Frank demanded—through commercial lending practices—that businesses achieve a profit.

Most institutional loans I look at now are requiring profit to debt ratios of anywhere from 1.2 to 1.5, meaning that if your annual debt payments are one hundred thousand dollars, you must show a cash profit of $120,000 to $150,000 in order to be compliant with your loan covenant. And even if restaurant owners don't go through institutional lenders, private investors have the same expectations of debt repayment and profit. So, restauranteurs must understand how to price their menus to accommodate the profit required to sustain investment and financing requirements.

Let's look at a couple of examples of market changes that could affect a business, and how to adjust for them.

Example 1: You are a coffee shop owner and your local city council decides it wants to ban all nonrecyclable plastics. Most coffee shops sell their coffee in paper to-go containers with plastic lids. The industry has figured out how to replace Styrofoam with recyclable paper cups in a cost-effective manner, but that little lid that keeps the hot liquids contained in the cup is made of plastic. As of the writing of this book, recyclable plastic coffee cup tops are very expensive, running about $0.25 more than the current non-recyclable option. The city council looks at this as a simple financial fix. Simply charge $0.25 more for each cup of coffee and you will make the same profit. Sounds easy, right?

Let's test the notion that simply charging $0.25 more for a cup of coffee maintains current profitability. Going back to my hypothetical example of a cappuccino's raw cost being $1.00, we will upgrade the direct cost to $1.25 based on using the new recyclable plastic lid. I know some would say, "Hold on, the plastic lid is a paper supply and not a part of the recipe." In a standard restaurant setting I would say you are correct. But as a coffee shop that serves most of its products in disposable containers, the cup, lid, sleeve and stir stick should be calculated as part of the recipe as it is essential to the production of the product. So, let's run this cost through our three example restaurant scenarios.

Step #1 Calculate the Overhead Factor OHF =COGS/ Total Expenses			
COGS	2,079,915	1,149,520	1,085,031
Total Expenses	4,306,653	2,552,639	2,046,896
Overhead Factor	2.07	2.22	1.89
Step #2 Calculate Breakeven Raw Product (RP) Cost X OHF + RP			
Break Even Cost (raw Product cost = $1.25)	3.84	4.03	3.61
Step #3 Calculate Retail Mark up based on desired Profit % BEC / reciprocal of desired profit			
Example at 10% profit (BEC/.9)	**$4.26**	**$4.47**	**$4.01**

In the first M1 store, the actual new retail price required in order to maintain a 10 percent profit is $4.26. In the M2 store the retail price should be $4.50, and in the M3 store the retail price should be set at $4.01. This changes the targeted COGS percentages to 29%, 28%, and 31% respectively in order to maintain the same 10% profit goal.

Now, if we apply the city council's logic of simply charging $0.25 more to cover the cost of the lid, the M1 retail price would be $3.70, causing a real loss of $0.14 on every cup sold. The M2 retail price would be $3.85, causing a real loss of $0.18. And the M3 retail price would be $3.50, causing a real loss of $0.11. For each of these stores, the retail price required in order to maintain the 10% profit margin for the $0.25 increase of the recyclable plastic lid is actually $0.80, $0.90, and $0.75 respectively.

The coffee shop owner would have to seriously contemplate whether the market would bear these costs. However, not following this retail pricing strategy and instead using the council's method, I guarantee that not only would the store fail to maintain profitability, it would indeed incur losses.

Example Two: What if labor costs rise? Let's consider what happens if the minimum wage is raised overnight from $10 to $15. In my pricing method, labor falls as an expense and not under Cost of Goods. If our three stores now average $10 an hour for labor, a $15 an hour labor cost represents a 50% increase in that expense category. Running this calculation for a $1 cappuccino plus a $5 per hour labor hike looks like this:

r-3M Sample Data

Step #1 Calculate the Overhead Factor OHF =COGS/ Total Expenses				
COGS	2,079,915	1,149,520	1,085,031	4,314,466
Total Expenses	5,573,389	3,279,464	2,676,588	11,529,441
Overhead Factor	2.68	2.85	2.47	2.67
Step #2 Calculate Breakeven Raw Product (RP) Cost X OHF + RP				
Break Even Cost (raw Product cost = $1.00)	3.68	3.85	3.47	3.67
Step #3 Calculate Retail Mark up based on desired Profit % BEC / reciprocal of desired profit				
Example at 10% profit (BEC/.9)	**$4.09**	**$4.28**	**$3.85**	**$4.08**

M1 would need to charge a retail price of $4.09, M2 would need to charge $4.28, and M3 would need to charge $3.85 to maintain a 10 percent profit based on the increased labor costs of $15 an hour. This would be an increase of $0.64, $0.68 and $0.60 respectively and would adjust the targeted COGS at 24, 23 and 26 percent. Of course, restaurant owners could accept making lower profit margins but then bankers and investors may be less willing to invest in your restaurant. Understanding external forces and knowing how to adjust your retail menu prices is the job of every business owner.

Once the retail market adjusts to these imposed expense realities, $15 per hour will have the same buying power as $10 an hour has now or $5 per hour had a decade ago. The important thing to know, especially for independent restaurant owners, is how to quickly adapt your retail pricing to absorb these mandated increases in expenses. As external forces arbitrarily upset restaurant profit models, the unprepared restaurant owner is the one who falls prey to attrition. As these market-changing policies are implemented, there is a natural culling of restaurants on weaker financial footing. The irony is, most of the politicians making the argument for $15 an hour labor costs, plastic bags, or whatever else suits their political fancies, do so to target "big" businesses, yet big businesses can afford CFOs and financial analysts to perform these calculations.

The dirty little secret no established restaurateur will tell is that the more government regulates, the better well-established business are protected.

The greatest challenge to running a successful restaurant is competition—not necessarily competition in serving good food, but competition on retail pricing. The restaurant industry is one of the most wonderful and ethnically diverse industries. There is nothing better for a community than a vibrant and diverse set of restaurant options. Landed immigrants from all over the world especially bring their own culinary delights.

For established restaurants, these local startup restaurants present the biggest threat. Because of their structure, innovative ethnic upstarts tend to have a much lower overhead and profit expectation. Thus, the specialty restaurants pose a real threat in competition, not only on taste profiles but on the retail prices they need to charge to make a profit. When cities and municipalities impose huge regulatory burdens and expensive variance procedures, they effectively weed out these wonderful and diverse fledgling restaurants.

In one recent restaurant project, the city code required a certain type of appearance for the restaurant we were building including the addition of a "living" wall of green vegetation and windows. The city code also required that garbage and recycling be housed in an indoor space. The total cost to meet all these requirements by the city exceeded a half million dollars. That particular restaurant is in no danger of ever having small, ethnically diverse and retail-price-competitive restaurants opening anywhere near it. Any other restaurateurs thinking of entering that market will be forced to charge the same retail prices as our restaurant, effectively eliminating it as a retail markup competitive threat.

My last words on how to survive the political landmines deposited throughout the restaurant industry is to understand that economics follows Newton's second law of thermodynamics. For every action, there is always an equal and opposite reaction. Any amount of government "tinkering" only provides a short-term benefit for its desired results. For instance, a $15 per hour wage only has a short time benefit to the employees who receive it. As I have proven in my profit models in this chapter, restaurants, in order to survive, have no choice but to adjust retail pricing to absorb the expense. An equilibrium between wages and retail prices will eventually be reached. And when that equilibrium manifests itself in the market once again, the politicians will call for a $20 per hour wage, and then a $25 per hour wage and so on.

Nothing I see on the political horizon convinces me that our economy will be allowed to naturally settle in to market-driven wages and retail prices, so for the restaurateur who plans to be in this business for the long run, I highly encourage restaurant owners to adapt the retail pricing model I have laid forth in this book. Nothing is more heartbreaking to the individual owners involved, and the community that loves and supports a great local restaurant, than to see that restaurant close its doors because it could not figure out how to adapt to politically motivated change.

The Biggest Decision to Make

You might think the biggest restaurant decision I have made revolves around whether to close my failing restaurant. Indeed, the agony and pain of deciding to close Portofino was intense. I spent many a sleepless night worrying about that decision, in fear of accepting my fate as a failed restaurateur.

Fear is funny that way. It invokes one of two raw instincts—fight or flight. Although these instincts are wired into our DNA, the options we choose in life have very real societal connotations. Heroes stand their ground and fight, cowards retreat. My decision to close Portofino had much less to do with the fact that the business was financially unsustainable. Conversely, I was far more concerned about being labeled a coward. I also did not spend a lot of time thinking about my own spiritual decay as part of the decision-making process. It was the fear of failure, being labeled a coward and branded as a business "untouchable" that truly weighed down my heart and mind as I decided to shutter the doors of my beloved restaurant. However, despite the drama and self-flagellation, looking back, it was not the biggest decision I ever made. The biggest one was to open the restaurant in the first place.

Opening a new restaurant is like starting a new relationship. In the early stages of the dating process, all we see are the endless possibilities—the early infatuations, the thrill of exploration and the clinging to the notion that this restaurant opportunity is our soulmate, the one that will last forever. Just like starting a new personal relationship, emotion—unchecked by a reasonable business plan—can draw the unsuspecting restaurateurs into uncharted minefields. The biggest decision restaurant owners or potential owners make is not whether to close a failing restaurant, but if they should open a new restaurant in the first place.

Understanding how to create a business plan, or pro forma, for a new restaurant is the key to making that crucial decision. This section of the book will discuss the key factors necessary to put together an accurate and realistic pro forma for a new restaurant. But be warned, there is no magic in the known world that will make a perfectly crafted restaurant pro forma—one that wins over investors and institutional financers or guarantees success once the doors are open on the new venture. Pro formas are merely models, predictors that if sales hit X and expenses hit Y, profit will be Z. If I had the power to create business plans that guaranteed financial success, I would not be writing this book. If I had that kind of wisdom, I would be comfortably situated in a Fifth Avenue penthouse suite with a constant stream of Wall Street dukes, earls, and duchesses begging for an audience.

There are many factors that are simply unpredictable when writing a restaurant pro forma. First and foremost is predicting sales. Although there are methods to better predict range of sales based on square footage or per-seat revenue, no business truly gets a feel for the actual revenue capacity until they open the doors. Variables such as competition, economic trends, and potential government oversight are nearly impossible to predict eighteen to twenty-four months out. The same applies to trying to predict cost of goods and inflationary pricing as well as quality labor pool availability. Already-operating restaurants have a difficult time managing these ever-changing variables on a month-to-month basis. Trying to nail them two years out with absolute certitude is nearly impossible.

Instead, what I will discuss is what factors are required to build a solid plan, how to spot the variables that, if not initially met, can prove disastrous, and most importantly, how to quickly analyze and adjust the business plan to avoid impending doom should any of the factors in the business model prove to be incorrect.

The Pro Forma

Over my restaurant career, I have looked at many restaurant pro formas. The more elaborate the plan is, with minute detailed descriptions of the restaurant concept and pages touting the restaurant genius of the principals, the more I worry about the veracity of the restaurant's potential for success. From my perspective, putting too many words into a restaurant pro forma usually means that insufficient thought has gone into the economics of the plan. Whereas most bankers and investors read a pro forma like they would a book, starting at the beginning, I look at the profit projections and then work backwards to test whether the assumptions will facilitate the projected results.

A solid restaurant pro forma should represent, to the best of one's ability, the true financial costs to open and operate the business as well as the realistic projection of revenue and cash flow. When I build a restaurant business plan, I keep it simple and to the point. I let the numbers rather than brilliant words tell the story. Building a successful restaurant pro forma is comprised of the following eight categories.

1. A brief description of the project concept
2. Listing the assumptions, such as square footage, number of chairs, menu price range, etc.
3. Calculating the pre-opening project cost
4. Listing the funding sources
5. Detailing revenue projections

6. Projected P & L statements
7. Projected cash flow
8. Return on investment statement

I have reviewed far more elaborate and detailed restaurant business plans with more than the eight points I mentioned above—plans that detail every nuance of a restaurant design and list lengthy descriptions of operators' vast experience. These *do not* guarantee the success of the new restaurant. I have reviewed plans that went into great detail about regional demographics, listing the number of households with median income levels. I have reviewed restaurant plans that include traffic patterns and local business populations. All this information is meaningless in a restaurant pro forma unless the future owners detail the precise marketing plan they are going to put into place to convert all of that data into customers.

Again, if a successful marketing campaign were all it took to ensure restaurant success, this would be an easy business. But those of us seasoned restaurant operators know the best marketing of a new restaurant is nailing a design and operation that stimulates the imagination and the five senses of every customer that walks through the door. A good location, with high traffic counts and a dense population base with high median incomes may help put butts in chairs but no brilliant marketing campaign will keep them there if the operators fail to deliver the experience that keeps customers coming back.

Therefore, I keep the description of the project brief and focus far more on creating a realistic financial picture of the proposed operation. Earnest marketing cannot commence until you have an actual product to market. Modern-day attention spans simply are not long enough to retain pre-opening marketing blitzes. More especially, for first-time or new concept restaurants, there is a danger that a pre-marketing campaign creates a false impression of what the concept will be—thus creating disappointment in the guest's mind if the finished product doesn't meet the advertised "hype."

Step 1

Let's begin with the description of the project concept. This is where the pro forma describes, in a very general fashion, the concept of a prospective restaurant. It is an "Italian," "casual," "quick serve," etc. restaurant with X number of seats located <insert city or neighborhood>. The restaurant will be open for lunch and dinner with the menu offerings ranging between $12-$25 and an estimated average of $28 per check. It is also important to include square footage of the proposed restaurant and note whether the concept is the remodeling of an existing restaurant or new construction. Savvy investors and bankers will very quickly calculate construction/ remodeling costs based on square foot and revenue projections based on number of seats and check averages. Like reading a prospective resume, if a quick scan of the project cost and revenue projections doesn't pique their interest, they won't bother reading through the rest of the pro forma. Make sure the key assumptions of the project are briefly outlined in the project description.

Step 2

When it comes to listing the assumptions, I break this into two categories. The first list of assumptions are the pre-opening project costs. These include the cost to acquire a property, construct a new building or renovate an existing structure, and the cost to design the concept, including architectural fees and code requirements. Also included in the improvement plans are the costs for external features such as landscaping, parking, and signage.

Step 3

Secondly, list the assumptions for buildout and tenant improvements. Include the cost of equipment, furniture, artwork, electronics, and sound systems, as well as technology such as POS systems, phones, security systems, and internal networking. The plan also needs to include accounting and legal services. A well-designed pre-opening plan includes the cost of kitchen smallwares, china, glassware and silverware. Most importantly, my pre-opening plan includes the soft costs for training labor and cash required to sustain the initial three months of operation. The number one reason most independent restaurants fail is undercapitalization. First-time restaurateurs usually fail to accurately estimate the costs to open the restaurant and sustain the operations while they build their customer base.

Step 4

Once I have stated the pre-opening cost, I then establish the funding requirements. This is the detailed description of where the funding comes from to meet the pre-opening expenses—typically a combination of landlords, vendors, investors and institutional financing. Whether the cash comes from investors in the form of equity or institutional loans, there is a real cost of the money that needs to be paid back in the form of interest or dividends. Calculating the cost of money is necessary to create a viable pro forma.

Step 5

Before a projected P & L statement can be produced, you must calculate revenue projections. This is generally done by using one of two methods—calculating the revenue by square footage, or calculating the revenue per seat. I run both scenarios to best understand where to set the initial revenue projections. If you are a first-time restaurant developer, establishing the revenue projections per seat requires having an idea of the type of menu you plan to offer, along with a retail price range of the offering. You then must calculate the number of expected table turns per meal period. Finally, calculate the average guest check per customer to come up with an expected revenue model. This is the most difficult calculation to nail for first-time restaurateurs, as predicting customer counts for a concept that has never existed is extremely hard. For existing restaurants, this process becomes much easier as they have existing data on revenues per seat and revenues per square footage to draw upon.

The restaurant group I work for averages about $22,000 per seat and $775 per square foot annually. These per seat and square footage estimates will vary widely based on regional economic factors and restaurant concepts. Great care should be given to ensure the business plan's revenue projections meet local standards and concept intent.

Step 6

Once I have established the pre-opening project costs, how the business will be funded, and a realistic revenue projection based on annual per seat revenue, a projected Profit & Loss can be built. I prefer to start with the expected revenue split between projected food and nonalcoholic beverages, and alcohol sales by percentage. If you already have an existing restaurant, you could model those percentages based on a known entity. For the restaurants I oversee, the revenue generally casts to a 75 percent food, 25 percent alcohol split.

Next, I establish real labor costs plus taxes and benefits. Again, with existing restaurants, following known labor percentages and existing salary history is a good place to start. If this is a first-time restaurant, great care should be put into modeling weekly and monthly schedules and attaching expected rates of pay to the model. It is important to add in payroll taxes and expected benefits. These are generally a percent of labor but vary from state to state and year to year. For the stores I oversee, this range usually falls within 11 percent-14 percent of total labor dollars.

Next, I establish the expense categories. I prefer the following breakdown of categories.

- General & Administrative Expense
- Direct Operating Expense
- Repair & Maintenance Expense
- Utilities Expense
- Marketing/Promotions Expense

You may notice Cost of Goods (raw cost of food and beverage) is so far missing from this equation. The COGS truly cannot be established until we round out the rest of the known or expected expenses. What I have listed so far are the parts of the Profit & Loss projections that take us down to Ordinary Income. But before I can estimate COGS, I must complete the rest of the overhead fixed and known expenses. These generally fall into the following categories.

- Occupancy Expenses
- Interest Expenses
- Corporate Overhead Expenses
- Incentive & Retention Expenses
- Depreciation Expenses

The layout of my preferred restaurant Profit & Loss statement looks like this:

Future M4 Restaurant Pro Forma

Ordinary Income/Expense

Income

Food & NA Beverage Sales

Alcohol Sales

Total Income

Cost of Goods Sold

Food and Alcohol Costs

Cost of Foods

Alcohol

Total Goods and Alcohol Costs

Labor and Benefits

Labor

Payroll Taxes & Insurance

Total Labor and Benefits

Total Prime Cost

Gross Profit

Expense
G&A
Direct Operating Expense
Repair and Maintenance
Utilities
Marketing/Promotions
Total Expense

Net Ordinary Income

Other Income/Expenses
Fixed Expenses
Incentive & Retention
Corp. Allocation
Interest
Depreciation
Other Expenses
Total Other Income/Expenses

Net Income

My preferred Profit & Loss statement is laid out in this manner so that Net Ordinary Income can truly be attributed to the activities of on-site restaurant managers. The categories under Other Income/ Expenses generally are not set by the operational managers. They do not have any control over lease agreements, debt service, corporate overhead, or depreciation. I also place Incentive & Retention below the line as our operational managers have very little control over how many employees opt in for health insurance and 401(k) programs.

I also include quarterly management incentive programs in this below-the-line category. The companies I oversee budget for 100 percent manager incentives that are paid out on a quarterly basis. Those reward payouts always fall in the following quarter. If a management team falls short of the 100 percent incentive payout in one particular quarter, placing this category above the line could in fact move the needle enough to achieve 100 percent incentive payout in these subsequent quarter without achieving ownership's objectives.

Now that I have established the Profit & Loss format, I then proceed to build a projected financial model starting with the known and expected financial data. I start by placing my expected revenue, split up by Food and Non-Alcoholic Beverage, Alcohol, and retail sales percentages. I then add in projected Labor and Payroll Tax Expenses. Next, I add in General & Administration Expenses, Repair & Maintenance Expenses, Utility Expenses and Marketing/ Promotion Expenses. Finally, I plug in the Fixed Expenses such as Occupancy Expense, Liability Insurance, Property Taxes Interest in Amortization, Incentives & Retention expenses, Depreciation Expenses and Corporate Overhead Expenses. Once these numbers are all established in my Profit & Loss pro forma, I apply the relating percentages of those categories as they relate to Total Revenue.

Now I move to establishing what COGS should be for the model to be profitable. Again, for simplicity sake, let's assume that we wish this new restaurant to produce a 10 percent profit. If my current pro forma Profit & Loss statement produces a 41 percent profit sans COGS, I have established that the total Cost of Goods expenses must be 31 percent (41%-10%=31%).

Here is where the rubber hits the road in determining whether your new restaurant concept can truly be a profitable venture. If I have done my due diligence by accurately predicting revenue and have been honest in modeling labor and expenses, the missing factor in deciding whether the restaurant will be a profitable venture comes from deciding if the remaining COGS percentage is realistic.

If I finish the model and show you a 25 percent Income percentage without the COGS number included in your formula, you then seriously have to ask yourself if it is realistic that, in order to achieve your 10 percent bottom-line profit, you can run a 15 percent Cost of Goods Sold? For most restaurateurs, and especially for first-time restaurateurs, that prospect seems unlikely. This scenario proves that the overhead costs are simply too high, or the revenue projections are not high enough to mitigate overhead. In this situation, the most detrimental move I can make is to artificially lower overhead projections or raise revenue expectations. That move may entice investors and bankers, but the result will also cause both to turn on the operator once the business fails.

Throughout my career, when I let my exuberance for a project elevate revenue projections beyond reasonable expectations, the results were always negative. Though it is the most challenging metric to produce, determining realistic revenue projections is by far the most important aspect of creating a pro forma Profit & Loss statement.

Steps 7 & 8

The last thing I do when preparing a pro forma Profit & Loss projection is to manipulate the revenue to show a 15 percent increase and decrease, as well as a 25 percent increase and decrease. I then run all the known expenses with percentages against those increased and decreased revenue projections to determine what the outcome would be if I missed or exceeded my expected revenue projections. This is an incredibly important exercise as it shows the realistic outcomes if that crucial revenue projection is not met. This also helps to establish the risk involved with opening the new restaurant.

If my model proves that the business cannot cash flow at the 25 percent less-than-expected revenue model, the risk may be too great, and perhaps this restaurant concept should be scrapped. If my 25 percent less model proves that it *can* cash flow, the only determination that needs to be made is whether the business can grow to the projected revenue model within a year or so.

If I determine that the new restaurant concept is viable, I then expand the projected Profit & Loss statement into a month-by-month model. In my forty-plus years of restaurant experience, I have never had a restaurant come out of the gate hitting every percentage metric including revenue.

I then model for the fact that my labor costs and product costs will be higher in the first several months. Depending on the concept, I may have higher initial marketing and promotion expenses as well. Realistically, modeling these very real deviations from the plan help establish an expected loss in the first several months. This real cash loss dollar amount is then added to my preopening expenses as funds required to have on hand prior to opening. For the first-time restaurateur, this underfunding of projected early losses is usually the first nail in their coffin. Not having this contingency usually puts a first-time restaurateur into a cash flow death spiral that becomes unusually difficult to overcome unless they very quickly increase revenues and control their Prime Expenses.

Now comes the most important part of putting a new restaurant plan into action. If you have any hopes of achieving your plan, you must establish the proper retail markup of your product to achieve that plan. If you expect your new restaurant to produce 4.4 million in annual revenue, run a total Cost of Goods of 28.7 percent, total labor cost of 35.5 percent, total operating expenses at 14 percent, and plan to produce an expected profit of $493,000 or 11.2 percent. (See M4 Expected Pro Forma.) The most crucial calculation is to figure out what your overhead factor is based on your expected revenue plan.

In my example, overhead expenses totaled $2,774,000 and cost of goods totaled $1,209,000, giving us an overhead factor of 2.19. Based on the plan, this means for every dollar of COGS there is $2.19 of allocated Overhead Expense. This means for every dollar of COGS, the breakeven retail markup would be $3.19.

Now, our plan calls for 11.2 percent bottom-line profit. To calculate the proper markup for your initial opening menu, you must first calculate the product cost of every menu item. I cannot overemphasize how important this is for a first-time restaurateur. Once you establish the raw cost of each menu item, you then must multiply that cost by the Overhead Factor of 2.19 and then add the original raw product to that figure to establish the breakeven dollar amount of that item.

Raw Cost × Overhead Factor = Break Even

Break Even ÷ (reciprocal of 11.20) = Suggested Retail Price

Future M4 Restaurant

Pro Forma - First Full Year - 2020

	EXPECTED	
	12 periods	% of Income
Ordinary Income/Expense		
Income		
Food & NA Bev Sales	3,292,972	74.5%
Alcohol Sales	1,127,125	25.5%
Total Income	4,420,125	100%
Cost of Goods Sold		
Food & Alcohol Costs		
Cost of Foods	1,004,356	30.5%
Alcohol	264,874	23.5%
Total Food & Alcohol Costs	1,269,231	28.7%
Labor and Benefits		
Labor	1,359,180	30.8%
Payroll Taxes & Insurance	207,745	4.7%
Labor and Benefits	1,566,924	35.5%
Total Prime Cost	2,836,155	64.2%
Gross Profit	1,583,942	35.8%
Expense		
G & A	137,023	3.1%
Direct Operating Expenses	229,845	5.2%
Repair & Maintenance	30,941	0.7%
Utilities	99,452	2.3%
Marketing/Promos	121,553	2.8%
Total Expense	618,814	14%
Net Ordinary Income	965,128	21.8%
Other Income/Expenses		
Fixed Expenses	257,456	5.8%
Incentive & Retention	132,603	3.0%
Corp. Allocation	176,804	4.0%
Interest	74,746	1.7%
Depreciation	198,238	4.5%
Other Expenses	22,100	0.5%
Total Other	471,889	10.7%
Net Income	493,239	11.2%

For example, a hamburger with French fries that has a raw product cost of $3.50 would be multiplied by 2.19. That establishes that the overhead on that product is $7.67.

3.50 × 2.19 = 7.67

You then must add the original cost of the product of $3.50 to give you a breakeven dollar amount on this product of $11.17.

7.76 + 3.50 = 11.17

In order to achieve your goal of 11.2% profit, you then divide $11.17 by the reciprocal of 11.2%, or .888. This would give you the proper retail markup of your hamburger with French fries: $12.54.

11.17 ÷ .888 = 12.54

If I were placing this item on a menu, I would set the price at $12.75. To verify that you priced your menu item to achieve your expected Cost of Goods goal of 27.87%, simply divide $3.50 into $12.54.

3.50 ÷ 12.54 = 27.91%

Using this method to price out your menu prior to opening is the best way to ensure your projected profit goals may be met, especially since you will have no data to determine the menu mix sales of the items on your menu.

As my theoretical M4 restaurant pro forma model shows, our total targeted Cost of Goods shows that we need to have a blended percentage of 28.7 percent. That assumes a liquor percentage of 23.5 percent in a food cost percentage of 30.5 percent. It is extremely important to keep these two targeted percentages in mind when you create your retail pricing. Once you've established your product cost and initial retail markup amount, each menu item should be analyzed to ensure that they are within the bounds of those two percentages. Because this theoretical concept has 75 percent allocated to food revenue, it is important to pay close attention to all food offerings to ensure that they meet the 30.5 percent target.

Sometimes, restaurateurs fall prey to menu mix roulette. This is where they create a menu that has a bunch of items at 35 percent food cost and another set of items at 25 percent cost. Then they let the customer's menu selection spin the menu mix cylinder in hopes that their 30.5 percent food cost is the result. From my perspective, this is extremely perilous for new concepts as predicting which menu items the guests prefer is nearly impossible. Until a history of menu mix preferences can be established, I highly recommend that new restaurant owners properly establishing all menu items to target the 30.5 percent cost of goods represented on the pro forma.

Rubber Meets the Road

But now comes the hard part. Very few independent restaurants come out of the gates meeting their first-year revenue projections. There is usually a monthly buildup in sales that occurs as marketing efforts and word-of-mouth take effect. It could take months or perhaps a year to build your business to the projected model that you used to price out your retail menu.

To ensure that my business plan can still provide cash flow on less sales, I then model the pro forma P & L at 85 percent and 75 percent of expected sales, identify the known fixed costs such as rent, interest and monthly utilities at set dollar amounts and then adjust my operational costs at a higher projected percent of revenue. There is a base minimum labor for operating a restaurant regardless of sales. As the sales decrease in my pro forma model, labor expenses as a percent of revenue will necessarily increase. This obviously creates a different Net Income for the 85 percent and 75 percent of revenue models. Calculating your plan at less-than-expected revenue at this stage of the game of creating your pro forma is crucial to establishing the risk of your new venture.

Future M4 Restaurant

Pro Forma - First Full Year - 2020

	85% of EXPECTED	
	12 periods	% of Income
Ordinary Income/Expense		
Income		
Food & NA Bev Sales	2,799,026	74.5%
Alcohol Sales	958,056	25.5%
Total Income	3,757,082	100%
Cost of Goods Sold		
Food & Alcohol Costs		
Cost of Foods	867,698	31.0%
Alcohol	229,933	24.0%
Total Food & Alcohol Costs	1,097,632	29.2%
Labor and Benefits		
Labor	1,277,408	34.0%
Payroll Taxes & Insurance	187,854	5.0%
Labor and Benefits	1,465,262	39.0%
Total Prime Cost	2,562,894	68.2%
Gross Profit	1,194,189	31.8%
Expense		
G & A	116,470	3.1%
Direct Operating Expenses	206,640	5.5%
Repair & Maintenance	30,057	0.8%
Utilities	99,452	2.6%
Marketing/Promos	112,712	3.0%
Total Expense	565,330	15%
Net Ordinary Income	628,858	16.7%
Other Income/Expenses		
Fixed Expenses	244,250	6.5%
Incentive & Retention	112,712	3.0%
Corp. Allocation	150,283	4.0%
Interest	74,746	2.0%
Depreciation	198,238	5.3%
Other Expenses	18,785	0.5%
Total Other	442,053	11.8%
Net Income	186,805	5.0%

Future M4 Restaurant

Pro Forma - First Full Year - 2020

	75% of EXPECTED	
	12 periods	% of Income
Ordinary Income/Expense		
Income		
Food & NA Bev Sales	2,469,729	74.5%
Alcohol Sales	845,343	25.5%
Total Income	3,315,073	100%
Cost of Goods Sold		
Food & Alcohol Costs		
Cost of Foods	777,965	31.5%
Alcohol	207,109	24.5%
Total Food & Alcohol Costs	985,074	29.7%
Labor and Benefits		
Labor	1,210,001	36.5%
Payroll Taxes & Insurance	172,384	5.2%
Labor and Benefits	1,382,385	41.7%
Total Prime Cost	2,367,459	71.4%
Gross Profit	947,613	28.6%
Expense		
G & A	102,767	3.1%
Direct Operating Expenses	198,904	6.0%
Repair & Maintenance	29,836	0.9%
Utilities	99,452	3.0%
Marketing/Promos	106,082	3.2%
Total Expense	537,042	16.2%
Net Ordinary Income	410,572	12.4%
Other Income/Expenses		
Fixed Expenses	244,250	7.4%
Incentive & Retention	99,452	3.0%
Corp. Allocation	132,603	4.0%
Interest	74,746	2.3%
Depreciation	198,238	6.0%
Other Expenses	16,575	0.5%
Total Other	422,163	12.7%
Net Income	-11,591	-0.3%

In my example, at the 85 percent of revenue model, my net profit drops to 5 percent, or $186,000. In the 75 percent of expected revenue model, bottom line profit is -$11,500 or -0.3 percent. (See M4 85 percent and 75 percent Pro Forma examples)

It is important to note that at each of these stages of less-than-projected revenue, the Overhead Factor changes. Whereas my Overhead Factor at 4.4 million in revenue was 2.19, my Overhead Factor on expected revenue of 3.7 million rises to 2.33 and my Overhead Factor on expected revenue of 3.3 million rises to 2.45. Because I priced out my retail menu based on my expected sales of 4.4 million using the Overhead Factor of 2.19, using that same pricing structure with the 85 percent and 75 percent of revenue models results in a substantial decrease of profit per item. Let's go back to my hamburger example.

At 85 percent of planned revenue, take the hamburger and French fries that cost you $3.50 and multiply by the Overhead Factor of 2.23 to get $8.16.

$$\mathbf{3.50 \times 2.33 = 8.16}$$

Add the original raw product cost of $3.50 and you get a breakeven of $11.66.

$$\mathbf{8.16 + 3.50 = 11.66}$$

Divide that number by 0.888 to establish the targeted 11.2 percent targeted profit and you get a suggested retail price of $13.12.

$$\mathbf{11.66 \div .888 = 13.12}$$

But remember, you priced out your menu based on expected revenue of $4.4 million and an overhead factor of 2.19. Although your hamburger will still return the same food cost percentage of 27.87 percent, this item will suffer a real cash flow loss of $0.58 each time it is sold.

$$\mathbf{12.54 - 13.12 = -58}$$

What about the same hamburger at a 75 percent revenue projection of 3.3 million? The new overhead factor at 3.3 million is 2.45. Hamburger and French fries cost $3.50 times 2.45 equals $8.58.

$$3.50 \times 2.45 = 8.58$$

Add back in the raw cost of $3.50 and you get a breakeven cost of $12.90.

$$8.58 + 3.50 = 12.90$$

Divide that by the initial .888 to achieve the original profit goal of 11.2 percent and we get a suggested retail price of $13.60.

$$12.90 \div .888 = 13.60$$

This item now suffers a real cash flow loss of $1.08 ($12.54 -$13.60). That represents an over 8% loss to bottom-line profit if all the menu items are priced using that same methodology at the full expected revenue projection of 4.4 million.

This scenario explains why independent restaurants lose money in their initial months after opening. In both cases, the restaurant operator achieves their targeted 27.87 percent food cost if they charge $12.75 on a hamburger with a raw cost of $3.50. But because the business overhead necessarily increases with diminished revenues, the breakeven analysis of each menu item necessarily increases with reduced revenue. In my original analysis and expected revenue, each hamburger threw off real dollar profits of $1.58. In the 85 percent of expected revenue model, the hamburger produced a real dollar profit of $1.09, and in the 75 percent revenue model, that same hamburger sold at $12.75, a real loss of -$0.15! As you can see in these models, menu items priced out at the expected model actually lose real money.

This is the greatest challenge for all independent and startup restaurant concepts. As I pointed out in my Portofino story, I was making my targeted cost of goods percentages yet failed to cash flow. I did not know back in 1999 how to fashion a restaurant model to absorb overhead, especially if projected revenue failed to meet expectations. This lack of overhead knowledge proved to be insurmountable in my beloved Portofino. I strongly encourage restaurant owners to take a serious look at actual revenue versus expected revenue of the restaurant models and if sales are not meeting projected expectations, applying the retail costing methods I have laid out in this book is the only way they can produce a profitable model without sacrificing the integrity of their concept.

For the budding restaurateur, determining whether monthly sales are progressing toward the expected revenue or settling into a lower revenue model is paramount. If you can see that your revenue model is growing toward what is expected, most restaurateurs will accept the early losses in order to maintain price continuity in their menu pricing. As you remember, when I constructed my original pro forma preopening costs, I factored in expected losses for the first three months. At this point in building your business plan, it is important to calculate those losses to ensure that you have adequate funds in reserve. If, however, the restaurant owners determine that the expected revenue model is not going to be achieved in short order, the only way to ensure profitability on a lesser revenue model is to set menu prices based on the new, known overhead factor. This can be the most difficult decision a new restaurateur faces as one is usually not prepared to raise prices on existing menu items three to six months into the opening of a new concept.

But as you can see, we are dealing with profits in pennies, and if the new revenue model proves to be at the 75 percent level of 3.3 million, that same hamburger retail price should be raised one dollar to $13 75. By doing so, the current revenue model will readjust your expected profit back to 11.2 percent based on the lower-than-expected actual revenue. Mathematically, there is no other option to ensure profit at this early stage of the business.

It is usually at this point that a new restaurant owner may choose to attack other costs. Maybe they attempt to lower food costs by buying a lesser product. More often, new restaurateurs address labor to reduce overhead costs. Both of these carry the risk of diminishing your original intent of creating an outstanding concept. Your customers may notice the lower quality product and be less inclined to return. We have all experienced dining in a restaurant where labor has been cut too much. Cook times increase if labor is cut in the kitchen, and there is nothing more dissatisfying than dining in a restaurant where the waitstaff is obviously scrambling to serve more tables because the front of the house labor was cut beyond reasonable levels. This "double-edged sword" approach to controlling costs to accommodate lower-than-expected revenues may hasten the demise of a new restaurant as guests receiving slow, inferior product with an overtaxed front-of-the-house support system may be first-time customers. If their dining experience doesn't meet expectations, it may be their last visit!

If I can offer any advice to first-time restaurant developers, it is to pay very close attention to these very real and mathematical realities when evaluating your new restaurant throughout the first year of operation. You mustn't be afraid to adjust the existing menu prices or produce a new menu based on now-known operational facts. To continue to operate the new restaurant with a model created at the expected 4.4 million level when realistically the restaurant may never produce more than 3.3 million is a recipe for either closing the business or infusing additional cash to sustain the business. Neither of those options please institutional lenders or investors. And, as I proved in my Portofino days, they take a tremendous toll on the restaurant operator.

Finally, no pro forma would be complete without calculating cash flow and return on investment. The example Profit & Loss projections I provided show theoretical taxable profit for my mythical restaurant based on the three distinct revenue models. It is extremely important to also model expected cash flow from operations. This is most commonly done by first calculating EBITDA (Earnings Before Interest, Taxes, Depreciation and Amortization) and then subtracting total debt payments (principal plus interest). From my perspective, understanding the cash flow position of a new restaurant is far more important than the bottom-line taxable profit. It is more important to your investors and bankers as well. *A restaurant model that shows a modest profit could still be losing cash if its debt service payments exceed EBITDA.*

This was another lesson I learned the hard way with my beloved Portofino. You see, when I put together my original business plan for Portofino, I was the guy who produced a highly polished proposal. It was filled with pages upon pages of flowery words about my background and my proposed restaurant concept, multiple colored charts and graphs and artist renderings of the project. It was so pretty that my banker left a copy of it on his coffee table during the entire construction of the project. Perhaps my banker thought that anybody who would go through that much time and trouble to produce a polished business plan could not fail.

I can tell you now, the one crucial detail left out of my Portofino business plan was cash flow projections. Perhaps I should have endured more discussions regarding the virtue of Snickers bars and cigarettes from my economics professor as, I'm sure, learning to model a business for cash flow would have followed in subsequent business courses at my alma mater.

Ignoring projected cash flow estimates on a pro forma is the biggest mistake all new restaurant owners make. And the reality is, in today's analytical and data-driven world, if a pro forma does not include cash flow projections, the lending institutions considering your proposal most certainly will. It is far better to know the answer to that question prior to approaching an institutional lender or investor than to have them perform the calculations and report back that your restaurant is a losing proposition.

Where Should We Go with Technology?

Let's review the history of technology in restaurants. My introduction to technology started with my father's Country Kitchen restaurant in the mid-1970s when he put in a behemoth white box computer (I believe it was an IBM) at the host station. Servers were required to fill out the customer's order on a preprinted stock card with lots of little circles. For instance, if a customer wanted the All American Breakfast with eggs over easy, bacon, and dry wheat toast with juice and a cup coffee, the server would have to blacken the circle next to over-easy eggs, blacken the circle next to bacon, blacken the circle next to the wheat toast, blacken the circle next to dry, blacken the circle for juice and blacken the circle for coffee. This process was repeated for every customer at that table. Once the card was completed for the order, the server hung the card on the wheel in the window of the kitchen. The cooks then performed the mental translation of all those little black circles into a cohesive order to be produced.

To be honest, having been a cook for my father's restaurant during this time, it was far more efficient to read the little black circles than to interpret the handwriting of a dozen servers. Finally, when the customer was ready for the bill, the preprinted punch card was run through the big white box, which made a series of hums and clicks, then some magical device from within started typed the order and tallied the total. The server then presented the card with a printed total at the table. The customer brought that same card back to the host station on their way out of the restaurant for payment. Again, the punch card was run through the big white box to open the cash drawer and receive payment from the customer.

I was fourteen years old when I experienced this first iteration of restaurant technology. I remember my father cursing this new "technology" because, like ice machines, it only crashed at nights and on weekends when the cost for tech support was at a premium. Thus began a long, fruitful career of loving and hating restaurant technology.

When I graduated from college in 1988, I worked part-time as a server and bartender for extra cash and the industry standard was NCR. This was a slightly smaller white box with a little green screen and a cryptic keyboard. Those of you who have been around long enough may recall a tattered booklet of PLU numbers that lay next to the register. While a handful of popular items may be found on the keyboard, most items required the input of the three or four-digit PLU number. I started dreaming about PLU numbers in my sleep. But the beauty of those more robust restaurant computer systems was that they remotely printed order tickets in the kitchen and tracked individual server sales, thus allowing for server banking. Paying tabs at the table greatly sped up the customer service experience and allowed for tables to turn faster.

When I opened Dunvilla in the summer of 1988, I sought to emulate the service standards achievable through automation. However, I didn't have the money to buy an expensive computerized restaurant POS system. I saw the value of customer service by utilizing server banking, so I sought a solution without technology. Each night prior to opening, we issued numerically recorded paper guest checks to each of the servers. The servers used those numerically tracked guest checks for the evening orders. Upon the completion of meal service, they manually rang the guest checks on an old pushbutton-style cash register and attached the receipt to the guest check. They presented the guest check at the table and collected payment. At the end of their shift they were required to total the receipts and remit payment to the manager. They were held accountable for numerically sequenced checks in their possession, and if a check was voided, it required manager's approval. The system was not foolproof and was extremely time consuming, but it achieved the desired customer service effect.

The 1990s saw many different companies enter the hospitality POS space. As previously mentioned, NCR was the dominant force early on. But, as the decade unfolded, Micros, Aloha, and Digital Dining were the leaders in utilizing PC/LAN server-based systems. At first, the code was written in DOS, but as Microsoft began to dominate the PC World, code writing switched to Windows OS. By the end of the decade, touchscreen technology emerged.

One of the automation objectives of restaurant owners in the mid-90s was to digitize recipe costing and sync the costing method with real-time inventory costs. Back then, as well as now, that was an elusive project, as most restaurants had inventories of well over a thousand items. Where most restaurants at that time were calculating theoretical menu costs in order to establish a desired profit markup, there simply wasn't software reliable enough to track the purchases and production costs of restaurant inventory. For what restaurant owners truly desired was the ability to calculate the theoretical inventory usage based on sales versus the actual inventory consumption based on physical counts.

As a result of this desire by restaurant owners, the decade of the 90s saw many Silicon Valley software firms enter the realms of the back office, inventories and analytics. In one of my positions in 1995, the restaurant purchased a robust inventory management software called Remax. The cost of this software was immense. Training and implementation proved to be four times more! But the Remax software handled purchasing, receiving, and inventorying products. For once, all inventories and current prices were held in the database, thus allowing for the creation of real-time menu costing. The Remax system also interfaced with restaurant POS systems in order to feed the daily product mix of sales into the software database.

For restaurant owners, having access to this type of analytical data had great value. For the first time, we could calculate a theoretical Cost of Goods percentage and then measure it against an actual COGS percentage. This greatly helped determine where waste, theft, and mismanagement of product occurred. It also helped define which menu items contributed to profit and which were drag. At tech shows, salesmen loved to show the splatter charts of the "work horses" and "dog's menu items that these softwares identified.

It was in the Remax environment of the mid-90s that I first learned how to interface to various softwares. The Remax system needed to interface with our POS system. A second interface had to be established with our accounting system. In this particular location, a third interface was required in order to push real-time costs into a retail pricing system.

Establishing these interfaces was incredibly complicated. Testing and retesting the pushing of data to and from these various softwares took months and required expensive IT consultants. But it was in this environment that I first was required to learn how accounting systems operated. Being responsible for overseeing the interface required me to understand not only what the operations management software was producing but how accounting software received and interpreted the data. So that I could understand where all the data lined up in those early flat file interfaces, I had to learn about credits and debits and double-entry accounting. This is neither the first nor the last time in my career in which I had mocked the people who enjoyed performing certain kinds of tasks like bookkeeping and accounting only to end up later in life performing those tasks myself.

As the 90s wore on, we saw incredible advances in software technologies. This era was known as the Dot-Com boom. Everybody and their uncle were into buying tech stocks, and the first wave of Silicon Valley millionaires and billionaires began to emerge. By the end of the 90s, most people had a cell phone and a Hotmail account. "We were flying high and wide and having a Big and Rich time![4]"

It was in this economically optimistic time of the late 1990s that I decided to build and open my own restaurant once again. Armed with my knowledge of restaurant operations and technology, I couldn't lose. Seriously, I knew how to cook, I knew how to schedule and manage employees, I knew how to set up and run the software that restaurants were migrating to, I knew how to design menus and wine lists and I was raised with the hospitality gene of enjoying serving others. It certainly was enough to convince my investor and bankers to back me. My training and experience led me to conclude that I simply could not lose. Somehow, I imagine General Custer said the same thing before Little Bighorn, with superior military training and high-tech weaponry at his disposal.

Unlike when I opened Dunvilla a decade earlier, I was armed with all the new technological weaponry the tech boom had to offer. When I opened Portofino in the year 2000, we installed a Digital Dining-touchscreen POS system. Not the sleek touchscreens of today—the old ones resembled a television monitor with a big box cavity to house the picture tube apparatus and a glass screen. But the touchscreen greatly improved service as it eliminated the keyboard and multiple keystrokes. The conversion from DOS POS to Windows-based POS was a great enhancement as it allowed for quicker order transaction times at the POS. It also allowed for more graphics on the screen, thus making it easier to identify menus and place orders. At the time of opening Portofino, off-the-shelf accounting software was also becoming available. They were relatively inexpensive and approachable by the layperson.

In June 2000 I opened the doors of Portofino Restaurant and World Market. It was a shiny new restaurant, with a shiny new Windows-based touchscreen POS, QuickBooks accounting software and a Yahoo email account. I was thirty-five and ready to show all these old restaurateurs how to run a restaurant, using the latest technology. However, fate had another plan.

The Dot-Com boom went bust in 1999. Two years later, 9/11 happened. Although that tragic day occurred in New York City, Pennsylvania and Washington DC, it had a ripple effect on the hospitality and travel industry that lasted for at least eighteen months, affecting tourist destinations in a very profound way. Finally, in 2001, I imploded in a sea of debt, self-delusion, and despair. Technology, after all, is just ones and zeros zipping around a silicon chip. Technology cannot save a failed plan.

For the four years between 2001 and 2005, I fell off the restaurant technology radar. After the closing of Portofino, I tried everything but running a restaurant. During this time of my life, figuring out where I was and what I was doing was akin to trying to figure out what Jesus did during his teenage years. My memory is spotty, and the records are incomplete.

In 2005, while still on my hiatus from restaurant operations, I worked as a salesman for a Digital Dining dealership. The technology available to the average restaurant was becoming more advanced and economical. QRS screens replaced kitchen printers. Menu and inventory software like ChefTech expanded onto the market and video surveillance, once reserved for banks and casinos, was now affordable for the average restaurant owner.

The Dotcom bust of 1999 had ferreted out the unsustainable upstarts, and in the POS world, Micros, Aloha and Digital Dining emerged as the three trusted workhorse systems. But they were no small investment. A typical purchase and install of a POS system for an average restaurant was in the $25,000-$50,000 range depending on the number of terminals and printers desired. These legacy systems also required extensive networking and in-house computer servers to operate. There were a lot of "moving parts" and complexities to the POS systems of that era. These complexities required extensive and comprehensive support agreements, thus the importance of not only selecting the POS system you wanted but also the dealer you trusted.

While I was selling POS systems, I got reintroduced to accounting interfaces. The dealer I worked for had developed a POS interface between Digital Dining and various accounting software packages. This interface created the daily journal entry for accounting, thus saving data entry time and errors. At this time, the dealer created software interfaces to payroll companies and key vendors as well.

The mid-2000s were all about data management. All these blinking and buzzing computer boxes were churning out tons of data. Visiting tech booths at the NRA (National Restaurant Association) Show was daunting and visually overloading as new software companies were showing the wide array of data analytic possibilities. But the problem was, the average restaurateurs did not have the time and resources to produce, review and react to the information. Only the largest restaurant groups with full IT support and dedicated "data" managers could utilize these new iterations of restaurant software. The next ten years became a race to make the monstrous data-producing technologies accessible to the average restaurant owner because they produced information restaurant owners desperately desired.

Though product mix sales and accurate labor costs had long been the mainstays of legacy POS systems, what we really desired was an efficient and accurate way to add real-time product cost to the product mix. This information would allow the coveted theoretical product cost to be compared to actual product cost not only among the broad categories of food, liquor, etc., but against actual product sold. If restaurants could actually determine the number of Jack Daniels beverages sold during a given period compared with a physical count, they could better manage their business with regard to shrinkage, waste, overpours or theft. Thankfully, menu costing software began to meet the challenge by producing effective and affordable solutions. These solutions also interfaced with the POS system in order to get valuable product mix sales into the analysis.

This is about the time I entered the financial side of restaurant operations. In 2009, I took a short-term consulting job with a small restaurant group. I was tasked with "opening the hood" on the financial operations and recommend solutions for the struggling business. Keep in mind, 2009 was the year of the housing market crisis, and the United States was slipping into a deep recession. The number one task I was asked to address was cash flow—in this case, negative cash flow. For you novices, negative cash flow is just a fancy term for losing money. Not to say that managing cash to maintain positive checkbook balances is not important and an art form in itself, but perpetual cash shortages becomes unsustainable for businesses of any size.

There were several easily implemented suggestions made to improve cash flow. One was to pay credit card tips on the bi-weekly payroll. Because of the large percentage of customers tipping service staff on credit cards, these restaurants were forced to go to the bank every day to withdraw money just to pay the credit card tips. As we all know, there is a two to three-day delay in receiving credit card remittances. So going in to your bank on Friday to draw five to ten thousand dollars in cash in order to pay out credit card tips over the weekend had a negative impact on cash flow because those funds would not be replaced until the following Monday or Tuesday.

But the greatest challenge the small group had was funding underperforming stores with revenues from successful stores. In retrospect, without having profitable entities to support the unprofitable restaurants, my job would've been unnecessary. However, it did require some restructuring.

First off, as this group grew from one store to five stores, each store was partially funded through conventional financing and equipment leases. By the time I arrived, there were eleven institutional loans and leases consuming a large amount of cash each month. Though the overall debt-to-revenue ratio was not extreme, paying these eleven loans and leases, ranging from 6 to 12 percent interest, took a large toll on cash flow.

Along with paying credit card tips on the employee's paycheck, I suggested consolidating the debt and refinancing the entire lot. At that time, the company was paying $78,000 a month in debt service. Refinancing the outstanding amounts at a more favorable interest rate would drop our monthly payments down to $23,000. I made additional suggestions about streamlining the accounting processes, producing weekly cash flow analyses and creating real menu costs and retail markups that would ensure more profitable outcomes.

Of course, at this time I just doing a two-week consulting project to identify weaknesses and suggest solutions. At the end of the two weeks, I presented about ten suggestions for the group to consider. After my presentation, I expected to be on my way with a firm pat on the back and a check in my pocket. Little did I know that this group would hire me as a long-term consultant to implement my suggestions. Word to the wise for all you would be consultants—don't make any business suggestions you're not willing or able to fulfill personally.

The first project we tackled was the debt restructuring. In normal times, this was not an insurmountable task. Lenders were always available to lend money to financially strong guarantors, but this project was occurring in the aftermath of the banking crisis of 2009. Dodd-Frank had been enacted, and ownership financial strength was not enough to win a loan restructure. Interestingly, starting a new business would have been easier to finance than restructuring an existing business in those years following 2009. But after renegotiating some vendor contracts and closing or selling under-preforming locations, a deal was finally struck, and the debt was restructured into a single loan at 5.5 percent. Additional cash of $55,000 each month went a long way toward righting the cash-strapped ship.

Establishing weekly cash flow models helped manage the expected revenues to cover major cash expenditures like sales tax, payroll, rent and debt payments. We had stopped the red ink and could now focus on the accounting inefficiencies. Our resources were still limited, but we began to develop better, faster, and more accurate accounting practices. We needed to get more timely financial information to the store managers. At that time, our company had two full-time staff members who did nothing but enter data and supply financial results. Store managers entered daily sales information in Excel spreadsheet reports and emailed them to the Home Office. We deciphered the information and entered daily sales into our accounting system. We also drove hundreds of invoices into QuickBooks.

In those days, we hired bookkeepers who could key in data quickly and accurately. But our problem was spreadsheet integrity. Store managers were not hired for their Excel experience, but to run and operate floor shifts. The spreadsheet data they entered was often inaccurate, and data transfer information was miskeyed or formulas were corrupted. I dubbed this era "spreadsheet hell." We set out to streamline the information transfer but remember—resources were meager.

We hired a brilliant software developer to create an interface between Digital Dining and QuickBooks. His software collected daily sales, labor and product mix from the POS and created a streamlined interface of the daily sales into QuickBooks. He also created an invoice batching system whereby store managers and chefs could enter their own invoices into his software allowing us to import the data once again into QuickBooks. The software engine was written in Microsoft SQL. The tool allowed us to more quickly import daily sales and imports into our accounting software as well as give our store managers more up-to-date purchasing information. It was a great improvement on the current system where the managers had to wait three to four weeks after the close of a financial period to get their cost of goods and labor results. It also saved countless hours of data entry at the Home Office.

I was so proud of this system that in the spring of 2016 I accepted an invitation to go to a Heartland Payment Systems sales conference and share our success. I stood in front of several hundred sales reps along with a couple of other restaurateurs and explained how the complicated system I had helped develop gathered data and interfaced with our payroll company and QuickBooks. My PowerPoint presentation showed the flow of data from one system to another.

While my system worked technically, it never gave us what I truly desired, which was more timely and accurate information. The work was still consuming all the time of my Home Office team. We still lacked the resources to analyze the data. Because the interfaced data was static (a digital snapshot of the data in our POS at the time of the interface,) I spent more time researching why a data source in the POS did not match the data source in QuickBooks. I became a detective rather than an analyst. Several of the restaurateurs who followed me gave presentations of how their operations were using more robust analytic tools and getting faster and more reliable results. Instead of leaving a conference feeling confident that I had achieved something spectacular, I left determined to improve our company's technology.

After my 2016 presentation epiphany, I packed up my accounts payable manager and my IT Manager and traveled to Chicago determined to find a better system. We spent two days at the NRA Show in Technology Alley talking to every software, POS and restaurant analytics developer. We emerged from the NRA Show sold on a product called Restaurant 365. Prior to our conversion our data flow looked like this:

Current Technology Configuration

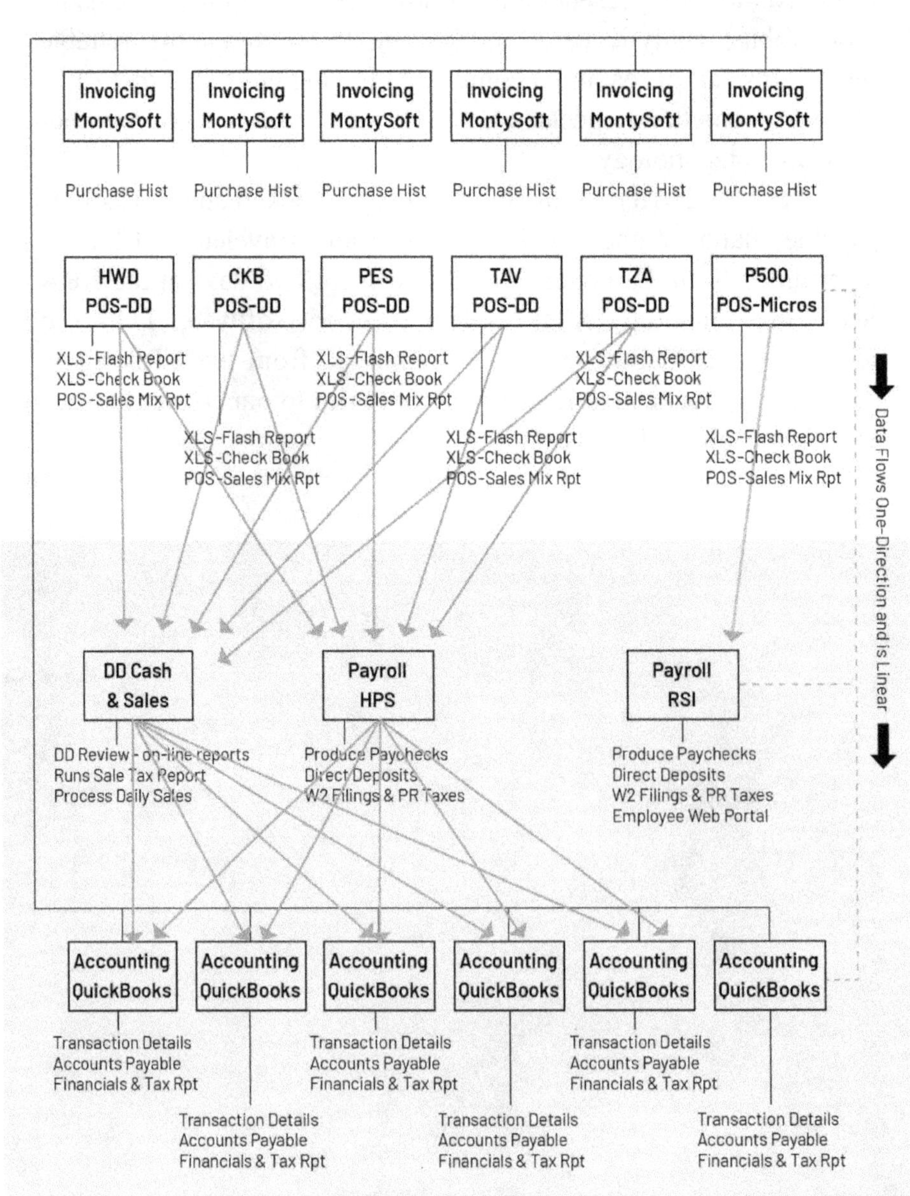

The goal was gathering all of our data into one system like this:

Proposed Technology Configuration with Costs

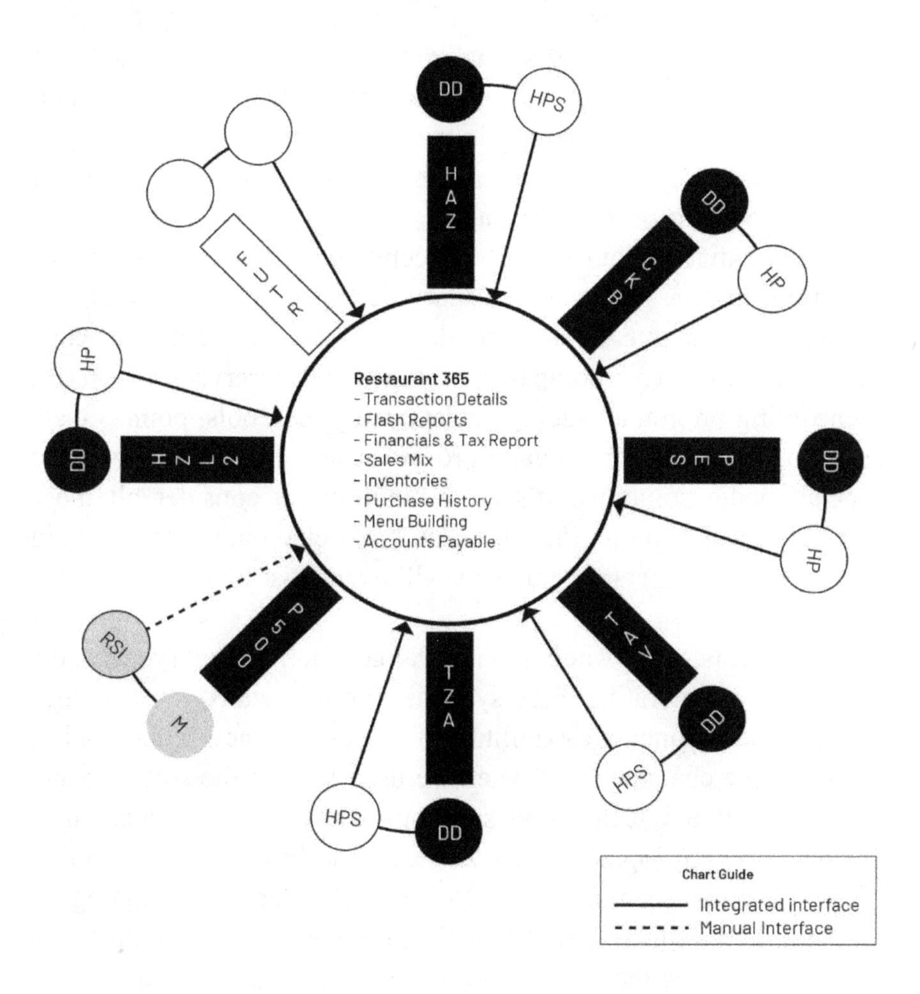

2015 Annual Technology Costs:

	Per Store	# of Stores	Total
Digital Dining Support	$1,500	5	**$7,500**
Restaurant 365	$3,446	6	**$20,676**
RSI - P500	$6,800	1	**$6,800**
HPS - NRG Stores	$7,867	6	**$47,200**
Total Annual Cost for Technology			**$82,176**

*One time Set up charge for Bank, Vender, POS and QB Conversion = $10,915 (or $1,820 per store)

What we desired was all the data residing in one system. Restaurant 365 provided that system. The software manages daily sales transmission, inventories, recipe costing and accounting all in one package. The good news was I no longer had to play detective looking for why various systems produced different numbers. If the information was wrong, it was wrong everywhere! But as a CFO, my job was to ensure accuracy in the financial reporting. Needing to be right focused my team on ensuring that the data was correct and that the tool was properly managed.

My advice about restaurant technology is to take an active position and assess your restaurant's specific needs and the resources available to analyze data. I received numerous calls every day from tech companies trying to sell reservation systems, scheduling programs, aggregate data analytical tools, point-of-sale solutions, gift card and loyalty programs, and enhanced web-based social media solutions. It's mind-numbing to consider all these technological opportunities. It's also more challenging to ascertain which of these upstart companies will even exist two or three years down the road.

All restaurant owners should evaluate their current systems, the efficiency of operating those systems, and the relative cost savings or revenue enhancing capabilities of prospective new technologies. Times have changed from when we used to own the software and hardware of our technology solutions. Now, virtually every new technology development is cloud-based and has recurring monthly fees. With this seemingly endless array of emerging technologies, separating the wheat from the chaff can be daunting, but it must start with anticipating the additional revenue or cost savings a new piece of technology offers.

Conclusion

Did I tell you my college degree was philosophy? Well, technically I graduated with a Bachelor of Arts with Distinctions in Philosophy. So, if you stayed with me through the anecdotes that led up to my understanding of the mathematics of restaurants, perhaps you may wish to linger a bit longer to be mystified by the philosopher who runs restaurants.

I wish there were words to describe the look on my father's face when I came home from college after my junior year and announced that I had dropped my business degree and would pursue a major in philosophy. My father, the son of a tombstone peddler, lifelong restaurateur and hotelier, did not have a higher education degree. Dad and I had many shared restaurant experiences, but we never discussed Plato's economic theory on how to run a city-state or the fact that every serious economist thereafter merely restates Plato's arguments posed in *The Republic*. It was the ancient Athenians, with brief success 2,500 years ago, who allowed the Greeks the leisure time to think about such weighty matters.

The closing of Portofino Restaurant and World Market had a profound effect on me. Unlike my first restaurant, Dunvilla, which I merely stumbled into upon graduating from college, when I opened Portofino, I truly believed I had all the skills required to be successful. When I was forced to shut the doors on my dream thirteen months later, I was absolutely dumbfounded as to how it could've happened. For the nextseven years or so, I continually searched for the causes of my failure. What had I missed in my planning?

Don't get me wrong. Initially, I was more focused on who and what to blame for the failure. I blamed the town for not being supportive. I blamed the weather for not cooperating. I blamed my friends for not supporting me, my addiction for forsaking me, and the gods for not protecting me from myself. I had put in all the hard work and long hours toiling for other restaurant owners, and I truly believed in my heart that the building of Portofino predestined me for success.

But the reality is, it was not the town's fault—they were indeed supportive. It was not the weather, nor my friends or even my addiction that led to my failure. It was ego and arrogance. In retrospect, people did try to help, and my loving God was always there for me even when I was not there for myself.

I honestly do not know why I was sent on this lifelong journey of being a restaurateur. Throughout my career, I have had fun and adventure, but also heartbreak and pain. When I emerged from the ashes of the Portofino disaster, all I knew was that I wanted to learn something from my experience. I wanted to gain something tangible out of my dashed dreams. Like the Phoenix, I knew that if I survived the public scorn, the bankruptcy, the divorce and my own alcoholism—if I worked hard to learn why I failed—my "rising" would not predestine me to relive a past life but would project me into a new life. For that mystical bird rises not out of ignorance to relive a past life but with knowledge gained to live the next. My journey through the restaurant wilderness was indeed an adventure, one consisting of green grasses in the warm sunshine upon my face. My career has allowed me to experience the magical, and yes sometimes exotic, locations. I have been fortunate to experience restaurants and hospitality beyond our great country.

I have had the privilege to not only experience the restaurant cultures across my own country, the United States of America, but of the world at large. My career has taken me to the unique culinary cities of New Orleans, San Francisco, Memphis, and New York to name a few. I have awakened in Denmark to be served Danishes—a treat my hosts simply call pastries. I've spent days wandering the first floor of Harrods in London. I've sampled the wonderful outdoor cafés of the Riviera from Genoa to Nice. I walked the Agoura of Athens searching for the perfect moussaka and dined in Paris, Munich, and Berlin. I have sat deckside on boats enjoying meals on Lake Superior as well as the Caribbean. I've had fresh lobster grilled for me on the tiny island of an Anegada Reef and enjoyed fresh guacamole on the beaches of Cozumel. In all these meals I have enjoyed, the experience, friendship, and purpose were far more memorable than the food and drink upon the table.

Without food and water, human existence cannot be sustained. There is a sacredness to the act of taking a meal that is all too often overlooked. To share a meal with someone is to share a life with that person. It is something in our society that is often taken too much for granted. We often shuffle from one event or activity to another, barely stopping for a quick cup of coffee or a meal on the fly.

If sharing a meal is so insignificant, why are all life's important events shared over a meal? How many times do we share a meal as part of sharing our life? Baby showers, baptisms, confirmations, graduations, engagement parties, weddings, job interviews, first dates, marriage proposals, anniversaries, and simply taking a meal with your family at the end of each day, it is not just the meal that sustains us. Whether we know it or not, it is the meal taken with someone else where we share our life that is truly self-fulfilling.

Those of us in the restaurant business are party to this uniquely human activity of sharing a meal. We see it hundreds, or perhaps thousands of times a week, as our patrons come into our home. All restaurateurs, servers, bartenders, bussers, cooks, and dishwashers play a role in providing this most sacred sharing of life experience we call dining. Too many owners disbelieve that a restaurant's true purpose is to provide the sacred meal and spend their energy chasing the business myths. The true magic of restaurants is setting the sacred table and being present for the time our guests are with us. And the math simply sets up the scenario so you, the restaurant owner, can continue to provide this life-fulfilling service time and again.

I believe wisdom can come from pain and suffering, but pain and suffering need not be a prerequisite for gaining knowledge. Learning from history, in this case my history, may offer the best way to avoid the most common mistakes that plague far too many people in the restaurant industry. I suspect that those who have felt the pain of trying to build a successful restaurant stand to gain the most from the work I have laid out in this book. I wish nothing but success to all who wander into this crazy world of restaurant operations—the people who wash the dishes, make the stocks, grill the steaks, service the drinks, greet the guest and manage the entire process. You are restaurant professionals, and I salute you for your time and dedication to an industry that is my life.

I leave you with a farewell blessing sung at the conclusion of every Minnesota Boy Choir concert. It is the sentiment I hold for every guest at the conclusion of my time with them. It is why we who choose the life of serving food and drink labor long hours to create and maintain the magic—the environment where our guests feel they can share their lives with us.

> May the road rise up to meet you.
>
> May the wind be always at your back.
>
> May the sunshine warm upon your face;
>
> The rains fall soft upon your fields, and until we meet again,
>
> May God hold you in the palm of His hand.[5]

Appendix

Profit & Loss

Sales
Food & NA Beverage Sales
Food Sales
NA Beverage Sales
Total Food & NA Beverage Sales
Alcohol Sales
Tap Beer Sales
Bottle Beer Sales
Wine Sales
Hard Liquor Sales
Total Alcohol Sales
Total Sales
Prime Cost
Food and Alcohol Costs
Cost of Meats
Beef
Chicken/Poultry
Seafood/Fish
Other Meats
Total Cost of Meats

Cost of Produce, Etc.

Produce

General Grocery

Dairy

Dessert

Bakery

Soft Drink, N/A Bev

Total Cost of Produce, Etc.

Total Cost of Foods

Alcohol

Tap Beer

Bottle Beer

Wine

Hard Liquor

Other Bar

Total Alcohol

Total Food and Alcohol Costs

Labor and Benefits

Labor

BOH Labor

Line Cook

Prep Cook

Dishwasher

Expeditor

Total BOH Labor

FOH Labor

Bartender

Bar Back

Busser

Server Asst/Runner

Server/Wait Staff

Host

Total FOH Labor

ADMIN/ Training

Supervisor

Management
Total ADMIN/ Training
Total Labor
Payroll Taxes & Insurance
State Unemployment
Federal Unemployment
Workers Comp
Payroll Taxes
Total Payroll Taxes & Insurance
Total Labor and Benefits
Total Prime Cost
Gross Profit
Operating Expense
G&A
Office Supplies
Computer Supplies
Postage/Shipping/Freight
Payroll Expenses
Merchant Acct/Credit Card Fees
Bank Charges/Fees
Total G&A
Direct Operating Expenses
Licenses and Fees
Menus
Medical Supplies
Janitorial Service
Linen/Laundry
Paper Supply
Janitorial Supply
Dishwashing Supply
China/Dishware
Glassware
Silverware
FOH Expense
Employee Meals

Management Food
Uniforms
Suspense Clearing
To Go Supply
Smallware/Kitchen Supply
Equip Rent/Lease
Hiring/Training Expense
Cash Over/Short

Total Direct Operating Expenses

Repair and Maintenance

Equipment Maintenance
Building Maintenance
Maintenance Contracts

Total Repair and Maintenance

Utilities

Electricity
Natural Gas
Telephone/Internet
Waste Removal
Cable/Direct TV
Propane Canisters

Total Utilities

Marketing/Promotions

Marketing

Advertising
Hard Media
Soft Media
Reservation Services
Promo Print

Total Advertising

Decorations
Music & Entertainment
Contributions/Donations

Total Marketing

Promo/Comps

Promos
- Promo Alcohol
- Promo Food

Total Promos

Comps
- Comp Alcohol
- Comp Food

Total Comps

Total Promo/Comps

Total Marketing/Promotions

Total Operating Expense

Net Operating Income

Non-Controllable Expense

Fixed Expenses
- Rent
  - % Rent
  - CAM + ins + taxes
  - Business Insurance
  - Property Taxes
- Total Fixed Expenses

Incentive & Retention
- Health Insurance
- Voluntary Benefits
- Vacation
- 401k
- Benefits Admin

Total Incentive & Retention

Total Non-Controllable Expense

Corporate Overhead & Other
- Payroll Checks not Cashed
- Accounting
- Interest Expense
- Depreciation Expense

Total Corporate Overhead & Other

Net Profit

Endnotes

1 https://www.brainyquote.com/search_results?q=socrates

2 Eric Clapton, “Let It Grow”, 461 Ocean Boulevard, RSO, July 1974

3 Minnesota Society of Certified Public Accountants, “Restaurant Accounting and Controls,” 2017-2018 MNCPA Professional Education

4 Big and Rich, “Save a Horse (Ride a Cowboy)”, *Horse of a Different* Color, 2004

5 Old Irish/Celtic Blessing with unknown origins

Acknowledgements

My many thanks to Maria Schrater to help me organize this book and breathe life into the stories, antidotes, and examples therein. I also acknowledge the efforts of Dan West who assisted with the overall book design as well as making the complex graphics understandable. Next, I thank Gena Steinberg for her marketing and branding efforts that continue to keep this work alive in the vast digital Universe. Finally, I acknowledge the thousands of restaurant team members, hundreds of restaurant managers and dozens of restaurant owners that helped form this book – your ideas, innovations and passions pushed me to become a better operator!

About the Author

Bruce Nelson's restaurant career spans over four decades and includes working every conceivable position within a restaurant. Career highlights include Catering Manager for D'Amico + Partners' Atrium Catering, General Manager at Cossetta's Market and Eatery, General Manager at Suite Life Catering at Target Center, Chef Instructor for Le Cordon Bleu and CFO of Nova Restaurant Group. He lives in St. Paul, Minnesota, with his three children and a yellow lab.

CPSIA information can be obtained
at www.ICGtesting.com
Printed in the USA
LVHW110238090223
738568LV00007B/7